DATE DUE

JUL 3			

A ... at
the bc ... ing
its de ... dge
spann ... go,
Franc ... ers
togeth ... ery
weddi ... and
back.

O ... ling
anniv ... the
hikin

C ... to
that ... ne
Abys ... lis-
cover ... for
the C

T

DEMCO

"The story they have told of their love affair with Grand Canyon is an absorbing and inspirational saga. The reader not only becomes acquainted with the Canyon, but with a couple who are in love with life--and each other. The Lines are contagious. You have a rare treat ahead of you."

Mike Swartz, Interpretive Ranger
Grand Canyon National Park

GRAND CANYON LOVE STORY

A True Living Adventure

by
Francis Raymond Line
and
Helen E. Line

Published by

WIDE HORIZONS PRESS
13 Meadowsweet
Irvine, CA 92715

Library of Congress Cataloging-in-Publication Data

Line, Francis R.
    Grand Canyon love story : a true living adventure / by Francis
Raymond Line and Helen E. Line.
        p. cm.
    ISBN 0-938109-04-9 : $8.95
    1. Grand Canyon (Ariz.)--description and travel. 2. Line, Francis
R.--Journeys--Arizona--Grand Canyon. 3. Line, Helen E.--Journeys-
-Arizona--Grand Canyon. I. Line, Helen E. II. Title.
F788.L495 1988
917.91'3204--dc19   88-84
                                                              CIP

To the park rangers at Grand Canyon National Park, a group of dedicated men and women who work as much for the love of the Canyon over which they watch as they do for monetary gain.

Contents

Foreword

During one of my regular geology programs as an interpretive ranger at Grand Canyon National Park, I asked the visitors who had gathered around me on the Canyon's South Rim, "How many of you have been personally acquainted with the Grand Canyon for at least ten years?" Half a dozen hands went up. "Fifteen years?" "Twenty years?" "Twenty-five years?" Then one voice called out, "Sixty years!"

I looked around and there under the shade tree sat an interesting looking rather short man in hiking attire, wearing a beret and a huge smile. Beside him was his wife. So began my relationship with Francis and Helen Line.

Later that evening at their room in Bright Angel Lodge, my wife Ann and I heard some of the stories of the Line's personal relationship with Grand Canyon; about his first hikes on nearly all the Canyon's main trails with his brother Winfield in 1923; about Helen's introduction to the Canyon, when she and Francis helped rescue three boys on the South Kaibab Trail; about their annual hikes into the Canyon celebrating their wedding anniversaries. In fact, they had just completed their 55th anniversary hike the day before.

Eight months later, during the time I spent with Helen and Francis on his 80th birthday hike to Phantom Ranch, they shared with me their love for this Canyon, for each other, and for everyone around them. I experienced their enthusiasm and zest for living. In everything they do they discover new adventures and surprises.

Francis and Helen are like that — vigorous, alive, reaching out for new knowledge and new experiences around every turn in the trail. The story they have told of their love affair with Grand Canyon is an absorbing and inspirational saga. The reader not only becomes acquainted with the Canyon, and this whole southwestern area surrounding it, but with a couple who are in love with life — and each other. The Lines are "contagious." You have a rare treat ahead of you.

Mike Swartz
Grand Canyon National Park

Introduction

There are individuals whose adventures with the Grand Canyon have encompassed a greater time span — as well as a greater space span — than is the case with either of us. But no two persons — no married couple, we believe, have through the years had a greater love for the Canyon than we. It subtly helped to draw us together before marriage. It has been a golden thread woven through our married life; we have had a combined total of 114 year's acquaintance with it. It is in Helen's native state — a part of her heritage. The Canyon and the areas surrounding it have been the scenes of many of our professional documentary film endeavors for more than 40 years.

We are not trained specialists in such fields as geology, archeology, biology, ethnography — areas of knowledge important to a technical understanding of the Grand Canyon scene. In certain respects, this has its advantages. Henry David Thoreau had no scientific training when he first made his retreat at Walden Pond, where he saw nature and the world around him in such fresh and creative aspects that all humankind has been enriched by the splendor of his concepts. His biographer, Henry Seidel Canby, says of Thoreau: "He knew enough of nature to see wholes clearly; (but) as the infinite details of life grew more complex to his understanding, his vision narrowed and shortened. Soon he was studying Gray, whose botany . . . made plant study possible on a sound scientific basis. After Gray, it became increasingly difficult for him to look at a flower except in terms of science."

We have to confess that when we look at a flower, we see beauty first and botany second, and when we gaze into the Canyon's depths, geology often takes second place to the grandeur.

While we are not Thoreaus, we feel that we have brought to our Grand Canyon experiences a refreshing variety of uncluttered concepts, sometimes less scientific than subtle, and often more poetic than ponderous. At the same time, we are deeply grateful to the scientists. Readers of this book who want specific technical knowledge of the Grand Canyon should consult the dozens of excellent — and vital — works pertaining to its varied scientific aspects.

For us, the Grand Canyon has most often been an emotional — even a spiritual — experience. It is a phenomenon of wonder. Its varied challenges have prolonged our years and it beckons as a goal for more adventures — both physical and emotional — as long as we shall live. In our relationship to the Canyon — and to each other — this is an authentic Grand Canyon Love Story.

The chapters written by Helen are so indicated. The last half of the book, from Chapter 24 on, was written by the two of us together.

This chronicle covers a period of more than 60 years; during that time nomenclatures, distances, and other features recorded on maps — even established "facts" recorded in books — have sometimes undergone changes. We believe that our story will add important information to the historical record, not only of Grand Canyon itself but of the whole extended area of which it is the focal point, as it has developed from adolescence to maturity, from plank roads to super highways.

In the years when we first ventured into the Canyon, visitors — as well as rules — were few. We took certain liberties then — collecting a few rock specimens is an example — which we would not take now. As unofficial guardians of the Canyon, we urge you to protect it, and to love it. We hope this book will help you in doing both.

Francis and Helen Line

I

Honeymoon Chariot

1920s

The rutted dirt road which years later would be known as America's "Main Street" — Highway 66 — did not even widen as it skirted the wind-bitten service station and general store that made up the business section of Peach Springs, Arizona. On our map the place stood out boldly, the only dot with a name on it along the map's thin wavy line, representing 90 odd miles in distance, stretching from Kingman to Seligman. My brother Winfield and I had expected a town. But it didn't matter. We weren't nearly as interested in Peach Springs as we were in its surroundings.

"Look," my brother exclaimed excitedly as he crouched by the dusty roadside near the store to examine the map. "The Grand Canyon must be only about 20 miles from here — at least the lower end of it."

Laying down my pack and faded bedroll, I stooped in the dust beside him. "Yeah, 20 miles, but just where will that get us? We'll soon be at Williams. That's where you head into the *real* Grand Canyon. Let's go."[1]

The two of us, hitchhikers before that term had even been

1

coined, and when the twentieth century was still only a wide-eyed youth, were seeking our first view of the Canyon, after having already traveled over 11,000 miles to reach it.

Cars on that lonely northern Arizona road were even scarcer than the area's population.

In the excitement of finding that we were so close to one of the major goals of our trip we neglected to stock up on food and water before leaving Peach Springs. By midafternoon our two-quart water pail was empty; the only food left in our packs was a pound of uncooked rice. No car had come by, in either direction, for over an hour.

"We'll go hungry and thirsty tonight," was all Winfield could say.

A shimmering black dot, no larger than a flyspeck, appeared far back on the desert road. It might be a car. Never before on our trip had we flagged a driver down. But we needed water badly. As the vehicle approached, Win stood in the road, making a signal that we wanted a drink.

A Ford truck, equipped with a home-built house body, braked to a grunting stop. We were soon making the acquaintance of George and Jane Eberly.

"We're almost out of water ourselves," George explained. "There's a little left in the canteen — enough so you can each have a good swallow."

We both took our swallows. The lukewarm water tasted more delectable than the sparkling apple cider which we savored each autumn back in our Michigan home.

"Can't we make room for them on the bed, George?" It was Jane Eberly coming to our rescue. George was agreeable and we were soon comfortably resting on a real bed with the long desert miles melting behind us.

"We're from Washington state. Moving to Cuba, New Mexico." From his driver's seat George had to raise his voice to a shout so that we could hear him above the clatter of the old Ford housetruck as it bumped and careened along the rutted road. Smiling at Jane, he added, "We just got married."

Winfield and I had some difficulty concealing our amazement. A few moments before, we had been parched with thirst. Now here we were, charioting over the desert in the traveling

2

Lunchtime for the honeymooners' adopted kid goat.

home of a couple of honeymooners. The Grand Canyon state was treating us well.

Although newlyweds, George and Jane had a kid — a small baby goat named Lily. The little fellow had been abandoned on a mountainside, nearly frozen to death. Jane had adopted it, nursed it back to health, and named it Lily Eberly. The young animal was now so full of life, so interested in the two newcomers, and so curious about everything both inside and outside the car, that the four of us sprinkled the trail with laughter all the way to Seligman. It was a jolly time.

At Seligman, we offered to leave our new friends, but they almost resented the idea. The four of us, plus Lily, camped that night a little east of Ashfork and cooked a meal befitting two joyous newlyweds on a honeymoon, and two hardy hikers on an odyssey across America. For over an hour, we talked, sang, and showed pictures. We heard about the way they had met, and what a fine wedding they'd had. They told us of their plans for New Mexico.

The conversation turned to us. "So you're brothers," George said for the second time since we'd been talking around the campfire, and I explained that Winfield was only 15 months older than I.

"What in heaven's name brought you way out here?" chimed in Jane as she rekindled the fire with some dead pine boughs.

"That's simple. We've come to see the Grand Canyon."

Winfield's answer proved to be not so simple after all. Around the glowing camp fire, we told our newly found friends the reasons for this unusual trip of ours and sketched in — as related a bit more fully in the next several pages — the highlights which had brought us to this moment.

Francis, 18, and his brother, 19, leave their Michigan home for hiking trip which will carry them to Grand Canyon.

5

II

Two Goals Accomplished

1922

Having graduated from high school in a sleepy Michigan town surrounded by cow pastures and lakes, we figured that college could wait. With our parents' blessing — so we recounted to the Eberlys — we set out to hike America's 48 states[1] and work our way as we went. Some of our objectives were hazy, but five principal goals stood out — the Rocky Mountains, Yellowstone Park, the Pacific Ocean, California, and Grand Canyon. Through geography lessons in school, and the reading of popular travel novels, these five scenic wonders of America had become part of our lives.

With our parents, we had made trips by train to the East Coast and the South, so were familiar with that part of America. All our new goals lay westward.

We hiked much, but we rode a lot more, with lonely truck drivers, homesick salesmen, farmers and ranchers, once with an escaped convict who pulled a gun on us (to see if we were armed) before letting us into his wheezing Hupmobile. A 19-year-old girl picked us up out of Mason City, Iowa. She said she was married but had had a spat with her husband. Giving us a ride, then telling him about it, so she felt, would make him jealous. We didn't wait to find out. We always enjoyed the company of 19-year-old girls, but preferred them less conniving.

When pocket money dwindled, we landed a job in the North Dakota wheat harvest, then traveled and worked our way across the Great Plains.

At Bismarck, North Dakota, a tiny ferry carried us across the Missouri River into the Rocky Mountain time belt. A large roadside sign struck us head on: "Mandan, Where the West Begins." Winfield and I both shivered with excitement. We were in a new world.

Cultivated areas became scarcer. The topography changed; the rolls and swells developed into abrupt buttes. Broad valleys were strewn with bare, massive rock mounds. It was a freakish landscape. We had entered North Dakota's Bad Lands.

A few days later, while enjoying a particularly long lift in a classy Nash which took us into Wyoming, the country made another sleight of hand change. Open range land spread on either side of the road. Once we saw cowboys rounding up a herd of Herefords. The horizons expanded even more on either side of us, but seemed to close in toward the west.

"Looks cloudy there ahead," I said. "Do you suppose we're in for rain?"

The driver of the Nash laughed, a little patronizingly it seemed. "Those aren't clouds, son. Those are the Rocky Mountains." The shivers which Win and I had felt upon crossing the Missouri River changed to goosebumps which seemed as big as those misty peaks looming in the distance.

By dusk we could see a whole range of well-defined mountain giants, with the haze of other ranges in the distance back of those. The sun set between two peaks which formed the eastern gateway to Yellowstone Park. Here, in one giant eyeful — or rather, a whole week of snow-peaked, steaming, geyser-strewn, grizzly-beared eyefuls — we would experience the first two goals on our list — the Rockies, and Yellowstone Park. After several glorious weeks of *seeing,* it took a month or so of *digesting.* Winter began closing in. Cold winds and snow flurries whistled around our ears. In the Coeur d'Alene Mountains of northern Idaho we found a job, working for two months in a silver-lead mine half a mile below ground, where the temperature never changed.

On the day after Christmas our feet began itching once more, and our next goal commenced calling. We cold-footed it for California.

III

Goals Three and Four

California is not a state; it is a state of mind. As we discovered during nearly three months — and well over 3000 miles — of travel, up and down and back and forth across Californialand, it is a state of mind so expansive and feverish that even its never-ending Pacific coastline is unable to wash away its exuberance. Almost immediately, California fever struck us. We caught it from a native son.

His name was R. E. Skinner. For seven hours — and 186 miles — his Buick Four swept us like a golden dreamboat from the area just below the Shasta-Trinity Alps, down almost the entire length of the Sacramento Valley, to Sonoma and the Valley of the Moon. We began realizing that this third goal of ours was a winner.

Throughout that journey, the famous valley of the Sacramento spread on both sides of us like the spilled contents of a cornucopia. Fields and orchards of growing food were strewn all the way from the distant snowcapped Sierra which we could faintly see in the east, to the low mountains in the west, which shielded this treasureland from the Pacific Ocean, which now became the next goal on our list.

Early that morning, as our California odyssey had started, we had told our benefactor that San Francisco and the Pacific Ocean were our immediate goals. In late afternoon, a highway sign at a crossroads caught our eye: "San Francisco, 40 miles."

"Are we that close? Just 40 miles from the Pacific? I can't believe it," shouted Win.

Our friend slowed the car, then stopped.

"Boys, I'll let you out here if you say so. But I think it would be a mistake." With the aid of a map he explained that he was going on to the Valley of the Moon and the Jack London country around Sonoma.

"It's something you just shouldn't miss." His gentle yet persuasive manner was almost like that of a father. "Besides, if I were in your shoes, before heading for San Francisco I'd certainly take the Redwood Highway up through the Big Trees. There's nothing like them anywhere else in the world. You can get your first glimpse of the Pacific at Eureka. The Big Trees are worth the trip."

I could never thank R. E. Skinner enough for that advice. It changed my entire life, and indirectly laid the basis for this Grand Canyon Love Story.

We followed his suggestions almost to the letter. The Jack London country, under his guidance, was uplifting and exciting. And the Big Trees, which we reached on our own several days later, were worth half a dozen such trips.

Early one morning, at Eureka, we stopped at the edge of Arcata Bay to wash up and shave. The bay was salt water, all right; we couldn't work up enough lather for shaving and had to go on. But this was not yet the ocean. We still could not see the Pacific. That was now our goal — the next to the last one on our list.

"The Pacific Ocean?" A friendly garageman echoed our query. "You just go on past Arcata a few miles, and there it is. You can't miss it."

We soon caught a seven mile ride, out of Arcata, with Roy Carr, who spent the entire distance telling us about his wonderful girl friend, Teddy, visiting out here from Texas. Just as he dropped us, in front of the small house where his girl friend was staying with the Gibson family, there before us stretched the Pacific. To us, it was as exciting as the Rockies, or Yellowstone. Our fourth goal was almost within grasp.

But not quite. An enormous cliff separated us from the shore. How to get down?

In a roadside ditch just beyond the Gibson house, a tiny stream of clear water was trickling its way Pacificward. Here was a good chance to finish washing and shaving. Two girls left the Gibson dwelling and almost at once disappeared into a concealed path which apparently led along and down that cliff to the shore below. Hastily cleaning our single razor, within five minutes we had found the path and were wading gleefully into the Pacific Ocean.

With a pocket knife we made a fourth small notch in each of our belts. Another goal accomplished.

IV

Color It Blond

To achieve any exciting goal is a thrilling experience. For two kids from rural Michigan, used to swimming in quiet, cattail-fringed lakes, to step out into the Pacific Ocean, which stretches all the way to China almost without interruption — that is far more than exciting. For us, it was magic.

It was so exciting, in fact, that we had only partly noticed that those two girls, who had emerged from the Gibson house and who had unconsciously shown us the way down that cliff, were still there up the beach a ways, watching these crazy newcomers make fools of themselves. When we saw them, we went up to explain our behavior. We quite definitely noticed them now. The older one — she told us her name was Helen Gibson — had long flowing hair as blond as the sea sand which stretched all about us. She was 15; her younger sister Louise was 13. They weren't too used to all this expanse of water themselves, Helen explained. They had just recently come from the deserts of Arizona.

Arizona. The Grand Canyon state!

"Tell us about it. Is the Canyon as grand as its name?" Now that we were standing knee-deep in the Pacific, the Grand

Canyon was the last unattained goal on the list which had catipulted us on this high adventure. Here was a chance to get firsthand information from a native of the Grand Canyon state.

"I've never been there," the girl replied, a bit sheepishly. "I was born in Arizona, but we never visited the Canyon. Isn't that terrible?"

For probably an hour we talked with the girls, telling them much about our trip and learning from them exciting things about Arizona. It was almost dark when they said they had to take off for home. Win and I headed along the beach until it came close to the road. A dilapidated barn, or shack (we couldn't tell which, in the darkness) was set back a short distance from the dirt highway. Even though it was still early, we decided to call it a day. There was room on what was left of the old floor to spread out our blankets.

But we couldn't sleep.

"Francis," Win said to me, "I feel the day isn't over yet."

I had the same feeling. Rolling up our blankets in the darkness, we made our way out to the highway, wondering whether we should continue on north a bit farther, or turn back toward now-distant San Francisco.

A car swung around the bend, its lights caught us for a moment, then it turned off toward the beach. Within a minute, two girls came running toward us. One of them was Helen Gibson; even in the darkness I could not miss that long blond hair.

"We recognized you when the car lights caught you." Still out of breath from running, she added, "This is my older sister, Thelma. Louise is in the car. And our cousin Teddy from Texas. And Roy Carr. We're going for a beach party. Won't you join us?"

Win and I exchanged glances. Our day was certainly not over. For two or three hours — all of us forgot about time — guitar music and song and laughter filled the evening air over the Pacific beach as we sang and roasted marshmallows, then talked about Arizona and Texas and Michigan and California. And the still elusive Grand Canyon.

The next day was Sunday.

"Why don't you come up to our house tomorrow and have

Sunday dinner with us?'' Thelma Gibson suggested. ''We get back from church in Arcata a little after noon. I'm sure mother won't mind.''

''Why don't you come earlier, and go into church *with* us?'' Helen Gibson interjected. ''Mother *really* won't mind, if you do that.''

That night Win and I slept on the beach, next morning scrounging around to discover some vegetables in a deserted garden near that shack by the road, then cooking them in salt water from the Pacific over a little fire there on the beach. The ocean water seasoned them perfectly. Here we had had our first view of the Pacific, we had waded in it, we had tasted its waters in our breakfast stew, but we had not yet taken a swim in this newly found western sea. That omission was remedied immediately and we just had time to get up to the Gibson house as the family was leaving to drive to church in Arcata.

With Helen and Thelma Gibson we sat in on a Sunday school class which preceded the worship service. The black-garbed minister presided at both, and his Sunday school lesson was on the prodigal son. Helen and I exchanged amused glances; was the minister thinking, we could sense each other wondering, that Win and I might be prodigals?

The minister even accompanied us back for Sunday dinner at the Gibson table, and it was sumptuous. Following chicken and generous trimmings, we young people all rode in Roy Carr's Ford up the coast to see the Trinidad lighthouse and whaling station. Helen and I, sitting in the back seat, talked more about the Grand Canyon which she had never seen and which Win and I would so soon be exploring.

''Now that you have introduced us to the Pacific Ocean,'' I told her, ''that Canyon is the final big goal on our list.''

From our encounter with the Gibson girls Win and I headed southward, to San Francisco, Los Angeles, and San Diego, then up and down and back and forth across the Golden State for more than two months. We experienced California and the Pacific in a dizzying variety of aspects and moods.

Now it was time for that Canyon.

V

Color It Gold

March 23, 1923. California had been good to us, beyond all expectations, but our final goal was still beckoning. Arizona and its Grand Canyon lay ahead. From San Bernardino we started walking eastward.

A pitted asphalt strip, just wide enough for a single car, was our pathway across the Mojave Desert to tiny Victorville, where the asphalt ended and real desert roads began. We were expecting to have to do most of this barren way on foot but the wonderful luck which had been with us throughout our California journeyings was still walking along beside us. Lift followed lift, a couple of them with old prospectors. Two days later, near Needles, the chocolate-coated Colorado River was flowing along just beyond our roadway. That river was the California-Arizona boundary. Its waters had just bid good-bye to Grand Caynon. We were excited.

But excitement ebbed with each mile, then gradually faded into uncertainty, and finally into misgivings as to what the Grand Canyon might be like, if it owed its life to this coffee-colored lackadaisical stream.

The wagon road crossed the Colorado, toward Topock on

the Arizona side. From the narrow bridge we had a direct view down upon it, a view as good as the turkey vultures could get, as they soared aloft. Our misgivings partly evaporated. The river looked better to us now — a wide golden ribbon of water caressing the desert as it slipped cooly through this bone-dry land. California and the Pacific were behind us; we would be surrounded by parched desert now for days. Any water would look good.

An aging truck with two men in the front bumped over the bridge and Win and I each gave the driver a smile and a cheery wave. He stopped and got out — a young fellow in his early thirties.

"Not much room," was his greeting, "but maybe you can pile in the back."

Dreams such as this do not happen more than once or twice in a hiker's lifetime. The back of the truck was filled two feet deep with California oranges.

"Help yourself to a couple," the man suggested. "There's some sandwiches in the sack, too. My partner and I can't eat anymore." He and we rearranged the beautiful cargo until there was room for us to crouch in this golden heaven. No one kept count of how many oranges Win and I peeled and ate. Had our host meant a couple of oranges, or a couple of dozen?

The men were headed for Oatman, Arizona, to peddle their load. To repay their kindness, we helped them sell oranges along the street, and gave them a little money in addition. Our consciences were bothering us a bit. Although I cannot remember the details, I am sure we must have dreamed of oranges that night. Next day, refreshed and enthused, we headed on toward Kingman and Peach Springs, and the ride in the house on wheels of our honeymoon friends, who had wanted to know about our odyssey which had brought us here.

* * * *

So interested had Jane Eberly been in our tale of adventure that she had neglected her chosen task of replenishing the fire. It had dwindled to a handful of golden embers.

"Reminds me of those oranges you were guzzling," she

said as she reached to put more branches on the glowing coals. "I didn't know that people could be that nice — to total strangers."

My brother and I broke out laughing. "Nice," I exclaimed. "Few nicer things have *ever* happened on this trip than riding with you two — on your honeymoon."

Win and I, later that night after we had gone to bed out in the pines beyond the dying fire, thought over all that had taken place since we had entered Arizona. Our first ride in the Grand Canyon State had been in a truck loaded with golden oranges. Our latest ride was with these beautiful people on their honeymoon, pursuing a golden dream.

Decision time. We had thought that Williams might be the best takeoff place for the 60 mile trip northward to Grand Canyon. But 15 miles farther along, toward Flagstaff, was another Grand Canyon road, leading 65 miles up to the South Rim from Maine Junction. "There's a lot of snow on the Williams road," a man told us. "You might do better going in from Maine."

Our camaraderie with the Eberlys had become so strong that, in order to share their company a while longer, we continued with them over treacherous roads and through snow-dusted pines to Maine Junction. Our roadside noon meal together — garnished with Jane's herbs on the salad, and Lily's antics in a snowdrift — was a very special goodbye banquet.

When the honeymoon chariot at last disappeared in the distance, Win and I turned northward toward the Canyon — and came face to face with a sobering problem. A few cars *might* have been adventuring up to the Canyon from the Williams gateway. But none at all would be going in from Maine; the road was not yet open. It was blocked by snow. Sixty-five miles of forced, cold-weather hiking lay between us and the last goal on our list.

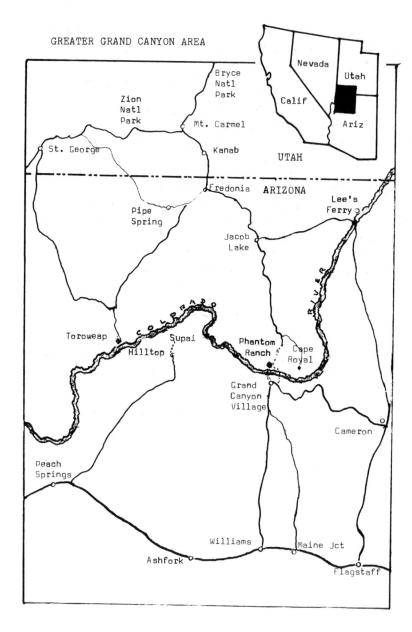

GREATER GRAND CANYON AREA

Nevada

Utah

Calif

Ariz

Bryce
Natl
Park

Zion
Natl
Park

Mt. Carmel

St. George

Kanab

UTAH

Fredonia

ARIZONA

Lee's
Ferry

Pipe
Spring

Jacob
Lake

COLORADO

RIVER

Toroweap

Supai

Phantom
Ranch

Cape
Royal

Hilltop

Grand
Canyon
Village

Cameron

Peach
Springs

Williams

Maine Jct

Ashfork

Flagstaff

Map of the greater Grand Canyon area covered in this book.

22

VI

Bare Bones and Antelope Rumps

My brother and I were lighthearted. Our packs bulged with 12 pounds of rice and provisions, procured at Seligman, and we could get water from melting snow. Dehydrated foods and trailmix had never been heard of in those days (at least for sale in stores in northern Arizona) and we always carried rice as lightweight nourishment in regions where supplies were scarce. The South Rim was just two days away. Good-bye Eberlys. Grand Canyon, here we come!

Snow and silence held our world in a soft embrace, broken twice by rippling music of small partly frozen streams, as we hiked confidently north from Maine Junction. We were Michiganders; we had seen no snow since shortly after leaving the mine in Idaho, and we loved its stinging glisten. Its crisp crunch underfoot supplied a marching cadence which carried us along in brisk abandon for 10 or 12 miles before we even realized that night would soon be closing in. By now the San Francisco Peaks--Arizona's highest--were our landmarks directly eastward.

23

These peaks would be like a compass for us most of the time we were in northern Arizona.

While there was still enough light to see, we made a clearing in the snow and bedded it with soft needles of fallen pines.

Knots from the pine limbs kept our small fire blazing cheerily, affording light to work by, warmth for our bodies against the gathering cold, and heat to cook enough rice both for supper and breakfast. Water boiled at a lower temperature, we found, at this nearly mile-and-a-half elevation, so that our cooking was slower. We spent nearly two hours preparing the two meals, writing our diary by fire glow, and making a comfortable bed. Long ago our "waterproof" poncho blankets had lost all claim to that name but we spread one out on the pine needles, carefully made our bed with the two cotton blankets of our bedrolls, spread the other poncho for the top sheet, and slept warm all night.

At least, nearly all night. Before the sun had quite decided that it was time to begin another day we were wakened by a mournful medley of wild, almost wistful music.

"What's that?" asked Win apprehensively.

I didn't know, but as we got our little fire going, to thaw out and heat our rice, we analyzed the recurring sounds and agreed that it must be the baying of coyotes. The first sunbeams were just groping their way through the pine branches as we packed up and were on our way toward the Canyon.

"NO WATER FOR 45 MILES." We looked at the sign beside our road, above a trickling stream, then we looked at each other. Seldom were we ever foolish in running even the slightest risks with our water supply. But the snow should provide all we would need. To fill and carry our two-quart aluminum pail would impede progress and we had almost secret hopes of making a forced push all day, even into the night, so that we could arrive at the Canyon next day. Taking long slow drinks, we headed on without water.

Win set a grueling pace which we held for nearly five hours. Our packs weighed over 30 pounds each; we had gotten wet in the snow, so that the forced hike without resting wore raw spots between our legs. Even though we had hiked over 1500 miles since leaving home, with hundreds of lifts from friendly autoists making up the rest of the distance, we were not used to continuous, long-distance, nonstop hiking in snow. Our high spirits began to ebb.

By afternoon we were getting disgusted, both with our progress and with ourselves. When it began to rain we stopped, made a couple of quick fires so each of us could have one to curl around, and rested for an hour. More slowly, we took up the trail again, but our calendar for reaching the Canyon was left wide open.

For an hour the drizzle continued; by the time it had ceased we were leaving the snow country. We had been hiking through pines but suddenly they ceased too; we were in open, high-level grassland. Ahead of us, grazing not over 300 feet away, stood an antelope.

The animal threw up its pronged horns, gazed at us intently, then started bouncing gracefully away. Twice it stopped, to wheel and glance back at these invaders of its domain. The sight was beautiful, and it cheered us immensely. We began watching for more. A mile or so away, off our trail to the right, appeared what we thought might be three or four of them, their white rumps visible as they caught the late afternoon light.

"Those aren't antelope rumps, those are patches of snow." Win sounded disgusted.

At the same instant, both of us forgot all about antelope and came to a sudden penetrating realization that we had left all the snow behind; those few patches well over a mile away were all that we could see in any direction we looked. Here was the place for another stern decision. Should we take precious time — and dissipate our strength — going two or three miles for that snow, or hope for more somewhere ahead? With a final wistful (and rather chagrined) last look at the patches of snow, we continued toward the Canyon.

"Antelope rumps, my eye," murmured Win to no one in particular.

Twice we saw other distant snow patches, but too far away to make it wise to seek them. Half a dozen times we left the road for short distances, hoping that snow might be concealed behind the north side of piled rocks. No luck. Then, perhaps a quarter of a mile off to the left, gleamed two patches of white. Winfield's legs were rawer than mine; aluminum pail in hand, leaving my pack with him while he caught up on our diary, I went snow-seeking. Drawing nearer to the patches, I knew something was wrong. The patches of white were not even in the shade.

A bleached skull and a few scattered bones grinned mockingly at me as I came closer.

That night, just before dark, we came upon some ice which had frozen about the roots and base of some pine trees and we sucked pieces of it eagerly until our lips became raw. There was still cooked rice left in our packs from breakfast. Camp-making was swift — and sloppy. We slept cold but well most of the night, sung to sleep by the wail of more coyotes. We were using the music of these animals, variously, as alarm clocks or bedtime lullabies, depending on our needs.

There was more ice next day, plus a little more rice. The going was tough, and we had almost no idea how many miles we had traveled or how far we were from the Canyon. In early afternoon numerous cattle became visible, dotting the open country before us. Soon, far ahead, appeared what might be a small lake or pond.

"Mirage," grumbled Win.

"This country's too cold for mirages," was my only comment.

Within less than half a mile, both of us knew that I was right. On the double — forgetting all about the raw places on our legs — we made it on to a rain tank, a muddy waterhole for cattle. Later we discovered some dead steers near the tank but, even if we had found them earlier, we would not have been deterred. Squeezing our last lemon — toted all the way from San Bernardino, California — into our aluminum pail of brown water, we had the choicest lemonade we had tasted since leaving home.

When a person has water to drink, it is surprising how unimportant food can become. Both of us were tired, but not overly hungry. Though it was still broad daylight, we made a comfortable camp by the waterhole, considering it to be even more desirable right now than the Grand Canyon itself. Yes, there was still some uncooked rice. We boiled a batch, in the chocolate-colored rain tank water, and had thick brown rice —

almost pudding — for supper. Win declared that when he got home he would never eat rice again as long as he lived. We wrote our diaries, checked our pocket calendar and realized that the morrow would be a day of triple importance, then went to bed. Not even any coyote music.

VII

Our Final Goal — Grand Canyon

Sunday, April 1, 1923. This was Easter Sunday. This was April Fools' Day. This was the day we would see Grand Canyon. We had joined the road in from Williams. A sign told us the Canyon was just seven miles ahead. By 9:30 a.m. we reached the park ranger station, registered and received a packet of free literature, then spent five or ten minutes talking with the ranger, gaining valuable information about all that lay ahead.

We were in Grand Canyon National Park — but still no Canyon. If this was an April Fools' joke it was the biggest one on record. All about us was a pine forest, on terrain as level as the cutover timberlands of upper Michigan. Since leaving the rain tanks of muddy water, all the land had been equally level. The largest scar in the earth's surface was hereabouts somewhere, but we bought groceries at the village store, hunted up the tourist camp, passed it up in favor of a secluded private place which we found out in the forest, all without seeing the Canyon.

This Grand Canyon was the only place on our trip — except

for Ashfork — where water had to be purchased, at the Santa Fe station. We borrowed some from a kindly camper, cooked a huge meal at our own private camping spot, ate and cleaned up, then headed for the Rim. We did not want our first view of Grand Canyon to come on empty stomachs.

Neither of us said much at first. We were not disappointed. We were calmly excited. But it was too hard to grasp — all at once. Perhaps we had had more difficulty reaching this spot than almost any other travelers since the auto road was put in. Our physical digestive systems were wrestling hard with the enormous meal we had just eaten; our spiritual and emotional digestive systems were wrestling equally hard with the enormity of this rock-templed, mile-deep, ten-mile-wide gash which lay spread out in mist-veiled serenity before and below us.

In late afternoon we entered the Hopi House, to see the fine Indian dances, then studied and took notes on exhibits about the Canyon's history and geology. We walked again along the Rim, giving our emotional digestive systems additional opportunity to work on the great abyss below, which was now turning purple and gold, with its mighty cathedrals and temples slowly being swallowed in shadows.

Back at our home in the woods, we cooked and ate a hearty supper, carefully concealed our belongings in the upper branches of a juniper tree, then headed toward El Tovar Hotel for an evening lecture. During supper, a light rain had started and as we walked through the woods it turned to powdery snow. By the time we entered El Tovar, both of us were covered with downy flakes. In our rough hiking togs, we felt a bit out of place with the handsomely dressed Pullman tourists in the El Tovar music room, but it was our government sponsoring the lecture, so we felt entitled to hear it.

The lecture and the slides were informative. To us they were thrilling, and we discussed them avidly as we walked, before bedtime, once more along the Rim. Soon, we quit talking. The rain and the snow had ceased. Easter Sunday always follows immediately after a full moon. From a bank of clouds, the Easter moon pushed its way into the dark sky and over the Canyon. Some powdered white snowdust was on some of the cliffs and cathedrals — turned by moonlight into white altar cloths spread over sacred altars. Our minds tried to grasp something that the ranger had said. The two thousand years since the birth of Christ, he had told us, could scarcely be counted as even one second in time, compared with the ages of those two billion-year-old rocks at the bottom of the Canyon. That first Easter, two thousand years gone, was only a second away, marked on the Grand Canyon clock.

The shafts of moonlight, clutched away then released by the moving clouds, touched first one temple then another, as though a ghostly spotlight were swinging the visible length of the awful gash below us. Once the whole Canyon was filled with blue light, but a minute later all was black.

The Canyon was filled with something else; there below was mile on mile, age on age, millennium on millennium, of far-stretching, unending *mystery*.

The mystery is there during daylight hours, but you don't realize it, and try to grasp and explain the phenomenon intellectually. Grand Canyon can never be an entirely intellectual experience. Nighttime diffused the geology and botany and paleontology down below. Paleolithic epochs blended with Cenozoac, hundred million-year-old layers merged with billion-year-old ones, and the dimly seen temples and cathedrals floated softly on a blanket of eternal *time*. The entire blanket was quilted with mystery.

We went to bed in another snowstorm. I could not sleep — not because of the snow, but because of what I'd seen and experienced on the Rim by moonlight.

I had begun — just begun, perhaps — to feel and discover the secret of the Canyon's greatness.

31

VIII

Catcalls at Phantom Ranch

The Grand Canyon changes with each hour, and with every visit.

This is in part because each floating shadow, each storm, each different angle of the sun or moon, as day and night play hide-and-seek with its temples and gorges, creates new shapes and colors and patterns.

The Canyon aspect changes, also, with the physical alterations, improvements, or destructions which have been imposed by men and machines. My brother and I first saw the Grand Canyon — and made our first descent into its open corridors of space — in the adolescent stages of its modern human development. Only El Tovar Hotel, the old Santa Fe rail station, the Kolb studio, and a small handful of other such landmarks were on the South Rim in early 1923. Except for a stretch leading to Hermit's Rest, no paved roads were in existence anywhere in the entire area. The privately controlled Bright Angel Toll Trail, from South Rim down to the river, was steeper, and shorter, in the early 1920s than it is as Century 21 approaches. Some of its more precipitous inclines have been eliminated or eased by stretching them out.

The toll must have been just for animals and riders; hikers were few and far between. No one was on hand to collect a fee from us. It was because of this toll on the Bright Angel Trail that the Hermit Trail was constructed, and the upper South Kaibab Trail later on.

There was no river trail then. To reach the just-constructed Phantom Ranch one went from Indian Gardens eastward over the Tonto Platform to the head of the Kiabab Trail (which did not extend up to the South Rim), thence down to the suspension bridge.

The present structure over the Colorado is, in a way, a third generation affair, built in 1928. The bridge my brother and I crossed preceded that one, and came shortly after the cable car which had originally been used in the crossing. The bridge we used seemed as slender and fragile as a fishing rod, swaying in the wind even without a person on it. Only one mule and rider could cross at a time. Win and I thrilled to discover its fragility, and found that by shaking vigorously at one end we could cause the other end, several hundred feet away, to shimmy in tune with our motion.

Phantom Ranch was still experiencing birthing pangs when we first came upon it in April of 1923; it had been started just the year before.

"You boys made it here all the way from Michigan?" the woman in charge replied in response to our oft-repeated explanations about this trip we were on. "My home was back there — in Indiana, just a few miles below Niles, Michigan."

"Niles? Just a year ago I was in the state oratorical competition there," spoke up Win.

It's a small world. This woman manager of Phantom Ranch, which now seemed to us (and to her also, as she later confided) like the most remote spot in America, had heard all about that contest where Win had spoken.

"A friend of our family was in it," she told us, then added, "Boys, I wish I could invite you to stay here overnight in our new facilities. But I'm just new here myself. The head boss is due in tonight. It might be against the rules."

A rather frequent turnover, we have later learned, takes place in the managerial job at Phantom. Years later, I had great reason to wish that this woman had still retained that position. No campground existed, so far as I can recall. The Ranch hugged the banks of spirited Bright Angel Creek, just above its convergence with the Colorado. Going on up the fault a short distance, we threw down our packs in a spot so exhilarating that it made us glad we hadn't had the opportunity of staying at the Ranch itself. Roaring creek before us, giant scarred cliff behind, tree limbs overhead, and a blazing campfire as our centerpiece, Win and I luxuriated in isolated grandeur.

As we were sitting around the fire preparing for bed, from across the creek came a piercing cry or call which sounded like the angry meow of a cat as heard through a megaphone. I had never heard a wildcat use its vocal chords, but since the rush of the stream would have drowned all ordinary sounds, I hastily concluded that these shrieks were not from a domestic animal. Crooking my head skyward I measured the distance from a low, overhanging rock above, to the place where my head would be in bed.

"This is a hell of a place to sleep." Now, I am a great hand to use slang but swearing just doesn't come naturally to me. In the early days of the century, "hell" was considered swearing.

Win had been less disturbed than I, when he heard the giant "meow." But when he heard my unexpected reaction, he hurled himself around in surprise. A few moments later the wild cry came again, but from farther upstream.

"Guess you scared it to hell and gone," was Win's comforting comment. This droll observation eased the tension. The night marauder did not bother us and we were lulled to sleep, not by wild catcalls, but by the wild galloping of Bright Angel Creek. Next morning Win couldn't resist a pun. "I really didn't sleep much," he lied. "I just catnapped."

On our return to the suspension bridge we physically examined some cactus blooms — the first we had ever seen — then spent odd moments for the rest of the morning trying to bite out or dislodge the needles of these Arizona forget-me-nots which had embedded themselves in our fingers.

We also gathered specimens of the rocks. No wonder the Canyon walls are mosaics of color when seen from the rim of the gorge. Green, brown, grey, red, white — our rock specimens

35

were like pieces of a broken rainbow.

Just as we started back up the South Kaibab Trail, toward its junction with the trail along the Tonto Platform, a rider on muleback overtook and passed us.

"Howdy," came his rather stoical greeting. "It's a bit steep. Have a good walk."

A rise of 1500 feet in elevation would be part of the next two miles of climbing. We knew it was steep, without being told, for we had been forced to put on the brakes nearly every step of the way, coming down the day before, to keep from catapulting over the cliffs. But Win's catnap had evidently refreshed his spirits.

"Let's beat that mule out of the gorge," came his challenge.

We did. The mule and rider rested several times; we did not slacken pace for the entire climb. Fifty minutes later we were sitting lazily at trail's edge, dangling our feet over a cliff and taking in the gorge view down below, when the mule and rider appeared.

"It *was* a little steep one place back there," Win called in greeting. For the next few minutes we and the rider became better acquainted.

We'd carried the tiny fragments of our rainbow rocks up that trail with us and now we took them from our packs and tried to match up their colors with all the tumbled ragged beauty of that granite gorge just below. The strata of the rib rock walls ran up and down, making them resemble Gothic pillars, except that they were far more rugged.

Green predominated — a rich impenetrable green whose somber luster suggested awful strength. There was brown, with a chocolate sort of darkness which merged in shadows to iron black. The greys had the sheen of steel. Mixed with it all was the red, like the red of a polished Michigan apple, which ran in veins with granite of pure white.

When the sun came from behind a cloud, the greens lost their darkness and shown like emeralds, the chocolate browns took on the gloss of a polished shoe, and the reds had the fire of a coke oven furnace. From our rock-ribbed armchair we saw not only the gorge; we saw and *heard* the river. Its white-foam tumbling rapids hurled echoing rumbles up to our ears. The mule rider was gone now. This whole stupendous panorama of scene and sound belong to us alone.

Here was the payoff for all of our climbing. If the Grand Canyon is one of the seven scenic wonders of the world, its granite gorge is an authentic eighth wonder in its own right. Travelers have tried to describe this view; artists have tried to paint it. In later years, Ferde Grofe even tried to set it to music. Words and paint and notes on a scale are either too florid, or too inadequate. This view must be experienced in the flesh. And soul. We had "Ohed" at it while making the descent, and we "Ahed" at it on the climb back out. This was the most precious gift that the Canyon had given us, thus far.

IX

The Music of Tonto Plateau[1]

Our day's hike, so we planned, would take us on the Tonto Trail westward over the Tonto Platform to Hermit Camp. The map showed this as a gentle, waving line. What the map did *not* show is what really mattered. The gentle waving line became a tantalizing path into a smorgasbord of adventures and scenic excitement.

Straight and level our route went for a few moments, then the trail started bobbing up and down over forbidding terrain, like a yo-yo, sometimes at fifty degree angles. Now it would cut far back around a branch gorge while a few rods across the abyss, as the eagle flies, the trail would mockingly continue on its way. Sometimes, though rarely, it would plunge swiftly into a gorge, curl its way along the bottom, then just as precipitously make its way out the opposite side. View after view of the river was now given us, and the granite gorge became a moving picture of color, with that word "moving" carrying double meanings. In one place, where morning light hit the granite walls, the colors seemed to echo and bounce into our field of vision. Win and I almost forgot about the difficulties of hiking midst all those echoes of grandeur.

There were other echoes, much less subtle. Even though we had been experiencing the Canyon-below-the-Rim for less than two days, these new echoes had become as much a part of this wild landscape as the granite walls or the switchbacks. Grand Canyon, we discovered, was a homeland for wild burros, descendants of domesticated pack animals which had been left behind by forgotten prospectors or explorers in some dim past. There were few places on the Tonto Platform where, within an hour's time, we were not able to locate a burro somewhere in the distance. And nowhere, throughout that day, were we for very long out of earshot of their clarion conversations.

Each animal spoke in a distinct key, but there was enough similarity to permit a general description. Their raucous caterwaul usually started out like the muffled sound made by a small boy exhausting himself on a tin circus horn. Then it increased in volume until it took on the tonal quality of a muted foghorn. By that time the Canyon walls were echoing with the strange music, and we were reminded of a factory whistle blowing on a chilly morning. Gradually the echoes grew fainter and finally died away. But now the receiving burro on some distant elevation had composed a reply and the strains were repeated, beginning this time, perhaps, on a long, sonorous note as a sign of "message received."

Sounds blended with colors all day long. In late afternoon, we made a great swing around a branch canyon, climbed up over a sharp rise, then headed down in a long series of switchbacks before leveling out (comparatively speaking) on the Tonto Platform again. Enveloped with visual and oral "music," we were tramping along, miles, as we thought, from our day's destination, when we heard another sound. It was completely different from a burro's call but even more out of place, even harder to believe. It couldn't be — yes it was — a rooster's crow. For a moment we were almost in shock, but only for a moment. I can never tell how good that rooster sounded. We had seen no one all day except that early morning mule rider, and although we had been having one of the finest experiences of our trip, we had walked and climbed and twisted and turned, and were beginning to long for a sight of Hermit Camp. The rooster crow told us that our day's work was nearly over. Topping a hill, we came upon several cabins in a setting of greenery. This was the Fred Harvey Camp. Our Tonto Trail experience was the finest in the Canyon.

But the day was not yet completed. Stopping only briefly at Hermit Camp, we set out on a brisk run down the winding trail to Hermit Rapids on the river, running the entire two miles to the "silvery Colorado" and fording Hermit Creek seventeen times in our joyful descent. After playing "goat" on the big rocks at the water's edge — somewhat perilously I must say — we retraced our steps a mile until we found a huge rock which suited our fancy as an ideal camping place. We were situated probably 25 feet above Hermit Creek, but Win wanted a bath so he slid down and, by holding on to bushes, reached the bottom safely. I had supper ready by the time he returned.

It was pitch dark before I started down for my bath. Something slipped and so did I. In the wild plunge which followed I lost soap, washrag, and towel, and my dignity. My fall as well as my skin was broken by some bramble bushes, but I did not stop until I rolled into the icy waters of the stream. It took probably 15 minutes for Win to retrieve me, but I had my bath. The canyon had torn our clothes badly so before we could start the next morning we had some mending to do.

The Hermit Trail was known as a good one and was described in the guidebook as having "only one steep stretch." That stretch, we concluded after climbing it, must have extended from the bottom to the top. It definitely seemed to us to be the steepest trail in the Canyon. Perhaps it was the high altitude, perhaps because we had had no breakfast, but at any rate we had to rest every half mile or so. Irvin Cobb, in his "Roughing it Deluxe," gave a far better description of the trail than the guidebook.

". . . Hermit Trail . . . is a marvel of corkscrew convolutions, gimleting its way down this red abdominal gash of a cañon to the very gizzard of the world . . . Alongside the Hermit, traveling the Bright Angel is the same as gathering the myrtles with Mary . . ."[2]

While stopped at Santa Maria Springs for a drink, a muleback party just finishing their lunch gave us some sandwiches and fruit which braced us up considerably. After numer-

41

ous forced climbs we reached the top, rising fourteen hundred feet in the last short portion of the climb.

Late that afternoon, in the Kolb studio built directly on the Rim overlooking the Bright Angel Trail where we'd started our descent, we heard Emery Kolb narrate his motion pictures and slides of the Kolb brothers' daring boat trip through the Colorado gorge.

That evening we went again to the government lecture in the music room of El Tovar Hotel. But this time we listened as old-timers. We had tramped all but a mile-and-a-half of the main trails below the Rim in this area on the south side of Grand Canyon. Upon balancing our accounts, we found that our Canyon adventure — both above the Rim and below it — for the two of us, had cost just four dollars.

It was worth four million.

After leaving Grand Canyon, Francis plies needle and thread to repair clothes which were damaged on Canyon trails.

Line Boys Finish 27,000 Mile Hike

Earn Own Way On Trip Touching Every State

FACE MANY HARDSHIPS

Howell, Mich., Aug. 23, 1923.

Winfield and Francis Line, sons of Mr. and Mrs. C. S. Line of this city, left Howell over a year ago, and began a tour of the United States via the public roads, walking, riding in automobiles, facing all hardships, meeting all classes of people.

Having graduated from high school the brothers determined to continue their education in the school of hard knocks, desiring to learn something of America, its scenic wonders, its people, and its working conditions.

"In our tramp we have visited the 48 states of the Union, have entered Mexico three times and Canada twice" said Winfield. "We traveled 26,741 miles, never once taking a train and never sleeping in a hotel. Nearly always we camped out under the stars." The older boy reports that he used up only two pairs of shoes while it took eight pairs to see Francis through.

The boys kept their own diary: in it are the number of miles they traveled, the makes of cars in which they rode, their experiences, the people they met, and all things of interest about the trip.

Their hometown Michigan paper chronicles the unique trip of Francis and his brother.

44

X

A Run to the River

1925

My brother and I were probably born with itchy feet. The love for travel which we possessed no doubt came as a natural inheritance from our father. He had traveled by bicycle (New York to Chicago and return, among many other such trips), by foot (twice climbing Pikes Peak), by horse and buggy (in central Michigan), and by steam train (to Mexico and to Colorado). He had covered the country. He is the only person I've ever known, for example, who visited San Francisco *before* the earthquake and fire. Just as the automobile era was dawning, our father collaborated financially with an inventor-genius neighbor of ours who built for us the first horseless carriage in our part of the state. That literally is what it was, with large buggy wheels and a whip socket. That vehicle wasn't able to make it beyond the village limits. It was some years later that our father bought a Buick Four, with which we sloshed through mud and sand and dust down to Mammoth Cave, Kentucky, chewing up seven tires on the 2500 mile trip.

Although he had once lived in the Rockies, had visited Yellowstone Park and California, and had gone swimming in the

Pacific Ocean, our father had never encountered the fifth one of those scenic wonders which had lured his two sons on their magic 48-state sojourn.

He had never seen the Grand Canyon, and yearned desperately to do so.

At the close of Winfield's and my sophomore year at the University of Michigan, in 1925, it was decided that our entire family — with Win and me as guides — would make a western trip by automobile, with Grand Canyon as one of the principal goals.

For me, there was a goal of much greater importance. Since returning from that year-long hike to the 48 states, with its Grand Canyon visit, I had begun a regular correspondence with that 15-year-old girl (who was now nearly 18) whose golden blond hair matched the color of the Pacific sands where I met her.

Helen Gibson had now moved, with her family, to Southern California. The Santa Fe mail train and the Michigan Central steamed on the week-long journey across the continent with letters between Ann Arbor, Michigan where I was in college, and Glendora, California where she was finishing high school. Airmail service was born during my sophomore year, which speeded up our letter exchange by two days.

An exchange of letters was fine, but I yearned to study her facial expressions as well as her penmanship. I wanted to see Helen again. My father wanted to see Grand Canyon. My mother wanted to see them both.

The day after Winfield's and my sophomore year ended, the four of us — the entire Line family — piled into a brand new 1925 Nash and headed west. Seven weeks, and five thousand miles later, traveling by way of the Northwest, we wheeled into Glendora, California.

But during that seven weeks the Gibson family had moved once again. There was no way that Helen and I could communicate during our trip, but she had left word with a neighbor that she'd be spending the summer out near Riverside with her sister and brother-in-law. They were living in an upstairs apartment, the neighbor seemed to remember, in a place called Highland.

Highland, out near Riverside, had probably a dozen places with upstairs apartments. No Helen. ''She's 18 years old. She has beautiful blond hair. You couldn't miss her,'' I pleaded to the occupants of every upstairs apartment in town. No one had ever seen or heard of such a person. I was more than depressed; I was outraged. Next day, while the rest of the family saw some sights on foot and by bus, I went out to Highland and tried all the *one*-story apartments and houses. The blond hair still completely eluded me. Desperately I wondered if this long journey would end up as just a frustrating game of hide-and-seek. Helen's straw-blond hair seemed harder to locate than a needle in a strawstack.

I was brought up on maps; had learned how to read one before I'd learned how to read. One of my greatest joys is to gather up a new set of maps and spend a Sunday afternoon surrounded by them as I peruse and study every nuance of their intricate cobwebbed beauty. After that second Highland fling failure I gathered together maps of California, Southern California, and Riverside County and began examining them with the intricacy that a sleuth uses in searching for clues on a ransom note.

First, on one map, a list of places starting with "H." Harlem Springs, Hector, Helendale (that was intriguing), Hidden Hills, Hidden Springs, Highgrove, Highland, Highland Park, Highland Springs.

Within two minutes, it was easy to discern that, of all the "H's" on my list, the closest to Riverside (Helen's neighbor had told me that she was staying close to Riverside) was a place called Highgrove. Within two hours I was out in Highgrove. Blessings for its smallness; only *one* second story apartment. *That was it!* Helen's sister Thelma, who'd been on that Pacific Ocean beach party, at once recognized me, and I recognized her. Helen had a summer job waiting table at the nearby famous Riverside Mission Inn. One hour later she was a waitress no longer. It was the nearest thing to a kidnapping escapade that she or I had ever experienced. We were on our way back to meet my folks.

They liked her, and she liked them. For the remainder of our stay in California she became a part of our family and we enjoyed all the sights together. Helen's hair was just as blond as I had remembered it. Our interests (we'd explored these throughout dozens of letters) were unbelievably similar, with just enough variations to expand both of our horizons. Having to go back, for

47

Francis' brother, Winfield, stands on plank road near Yuma, Arizona, on which the Lines traveled from California to Grand Canyon in 1925.

48

Wooden platforms marked with a post made passing possible on the one-way plank road across the sand dunes.

the next couple of years, to communicating solely by writing, would be hard. But now we were no longer visual strangers. We had explored each other's personalities — in reality as well as in writing. It would be hard to say good-bye — except that we both somehow felt it wasn't a final farewell. On a moon-filled, starspangled night, at the foot of those steps leading to the Highgrove second story apartment, we parted for another two years. After 1 a.m. that night, in our auto court, I wrote her a letter — the first of several hundred before we would meet again.

A few days later, the Line family arrived at Grand Canyon. It pains me to write this (and I realize now that it was only partially true) but for the first and only time in my life the Grand Canyon, on this visit, was an anticlimax. My heart was somewhere else.

Only one thing, for certain, remains vividly in my memory. Win and I started out at 5 in the morning on a hot August day, ran all the way down Bright Angel Trail to the Colorado River, spent 45 minutes taking a swim and jumping the giant rocks, then ran back up to the South Rim. Time: six hours, round trip. Winfield lost 11 pounds in those six hours; I lost 12. The run also helped ease my feelings of loneliness. Next day, our leg muscles ached as though they had been pounded with mallets. The aching of my leg muscles lasted only two days. The pounding and aching around the muscles of my heart lasted for nearly two years, until Helen and I met again, a long, long ways in the future.

That — with *her* introduction to Grand Canyon — is her story to tell.

XI

Grand Canyon Initiation
by Helen

1931

Arizona is not a place between carefully drawn boundaries
on a neatly colored map. Arizona, for the people who live there,
is an experience — an ever-growing sensation of expanding
horizons stretching between haphazardly strewn mountains, bot-
tomless canyons, and color-crazy forests and deserts which
swallow up space, and seem to go on forever. For a person who
was *born and raised* in Arizona, this part of the world is even
more expansive, especially if that birthing and raising happened
on a 400-square mile cattle ranch, which took my father and his
cowboys a day or more just to ride across in any direction, while
playing nursemaid to 10,000 head of cattle.

My actual birthing was in a house in Globe. Papa's two
enormous ranches were somewhat south of there, and it was on
the ranch that we spent much of our time and where nearly all of
my early memories are lodged. All of the Gibson offspring were
daughters — the eight Gibson girls of Globe, we were called —
but that did not stop us from riding the range. I was the seventh
child. My older sisters were full-fledged "coyboys," and could
ride with the best of the cowpunchers. Mae, our oldest sister,

51

often went with papa and the other cowboys to deliver cattle to the Apache Indians far to the north. By the time I came along, papa had probably given up all thought (or at least had given up hope) of having a son, and he had been too occupied teaching the tricks of the ranching trade to my older sisters to be able to take on a new pupil. But I *did* learn to ride really well. Papa always cautioned me, however, that if I should fall behind and become lost while riding along with the others, I should just give the horse the reins and he would take me back to the ranch. That happened to me once. I remembered my instructions, and did just that!

Albert and Rose Gibson, with their first babe (my oldest sister, Mae), came by covered wagon from New Mexico. Mama and papa, with their separate families, had come by covered wagon from Texas to New Mexico — papa from the Hill Country, and mama from the Galveston area. They had met at a cowboy dance. Hard times in New Mexico gave this new couple an excuse to move farther on — and Globe became their destination.

Hard times came again while I was still a young girl. Papa sold his two ranches and transferred to what must have seemed a "tiny tiddledywink" of land — just a 250 acre ranch northeast of early day Phoenix.

There were more hard times, and papa sold that ranch a few years later; financially speaking he probably sold it too soon. That 250 acre spread is now part of one of the wealthiest cities in North America — Scottsdale, Arizona. The old ranch house still stands, on Hayden Road, an historic architectural landmark.

Few persons have ever had a father more understanding and considerate, more "Christian" in the true sense of that word, than I. Just one thing I had held against him. We were Arizonans. Yet he never took me, or any of our family, to see Grand Canyon National Park.

For years I had secretly wondered about this. But then I made a discovery. When I was born — and for some years after — there *was* no Grand Canyon National Park. In fact, Arizona — the Grand Canyon State — did not exist. At the time of my birth, Arizona was a territory.

Grand Canyon was controlled in those days by a prospector — at least the trail down to the bottom had been claimed by one

Helen's former home on a 250-acre ranch in what is now Scottsdale, Arizona.

— who charged a fee for anyone wanting to hazard a descent below the Rim. The Grand Canyon, in my father's early cattle ranching days, was — for most Arizonans — just an extra wide gap in the earth. It probably never even crossed papa's mind to take us there.

He might eventually have taken us to the Canyon. But by the time the concept seemed plausable (of course it *was* several hundred miles from Globe to the South Rim, over wretched roads) we had to move yet again.

This time to Driggs, Idaho, at the foot of the Grand Tetons. Thank goodness that did not last long. Thin-blooded Arizonans, used to searing desert heat, are not acclimated to 30 and 40 below zero Idaho winters. One such ice-packed, snowdrifted winter was enough, although our reason for having to depart was a sad one. Papa was appointed executor of the estate of his brother, who had died over near Arcata, on the coast. We moved to northern California, to a house overlooking the Pacific beach — where Francis and I first met.

To that query which Francis and his brother had put to me that January day, "Tell us about Grand Canyon," I had had to confess my ignorance of it all.

Shortly after his first Grand Canyon visit, in which he and Winfield hiked nearly every trail below the Rim, he had written me a long descriptive, mouth-watering letter about the Canyon's lure.

Another such letter came after he and his brother had run down to the Colorado River from the South Rim.

After that, his letters were filled with other things than descriptions and impressions of the Canyon. They were filled with loneliness, and a whole series of such letters finally wore down my resistance; I quit college at Santa Barbara State and went back to visit his family in Michigan. We could be together at last.

Just before the time came for me to return to California — on May 1, 1927 — we became engaged.

One year later (I returned to Michigan for the event, since Francis was just finishing college and had also started a business with his brother, which he could not leave) — on May 1, 1928, we were married.

It was just like Francis; he wondered if the ceremony could be at 7 o'clock in the morning, so we could get an early start for our honeymoon trip to the Mammoth Caves and the Lincoln country of Kentucky. A year and a half after that our business was sold to Winfield. Francis and I moved to California on Oct. 29, 1929, and we rented a house in the small city of Ontario. Next day the stock market crashed, and the great depression began.

Depressions did not bother us — then or now. We began early learning to live simply. In 1931, with a thousand dollars from the money which Winfield had paid in buying out our share of the business, we started on a trip which would take us across America and up to Montreal by car, across the Atlantic by ship, and across Europe and North Africa, by train. Two hundred dollars was still in our purse upon our return seven months later.

On that trip we took in the sights of our own land, we saw most of the castles and cathedrals of England and the continent, we visited the mysterious walled city of Carcassonne, journeyed by narrow gauge from Brig, Switzerland up to Zermatt, a mountain-enclosed village, then walked along the mountainside until we had a glorious view of the Matterhorn; we explored remote ice-scarred passes of the Alps, and crisscrossed the Mediterranean Sea from Marseille to Majorca to Algiers in search of its exotic wonders. And as a native Arizonan, I am proud and joyous to say that one of the grandest experiences of them all was my initial visit to Grand Canyon. That was almost the first great sight we experienced after leaving home — and the last upon returning. It was among the world's best. I said a prayer of thanks to my father that he had not taken me there before; I was able to see and experience it, for the first time, with Francis.

As usual, whenever anyone is with him, things at once began to happen.

XII

Rescue Below The Rim
by Helen

1931

Most visitors to Grand Canyon view it as a spectacle, a tourist experience, even perhaps a "show of shows."

I looked at its sweeping depths with a pair of eyes, and felt its mysterious spell with a sense of emotions that most others might never bring to the scene. I somehow looked at it as an extension of all the mountain wonders and all the desert silences and all the rangeland vastnesses of my native Arizona. One of course can never see and discover *all* that Grand Canyon means, but I admit that I probably reversed that process; doubtless I saw it — and projected characteristics into it — which the Grand Canyon may not have possessed.

Francis said my feelings for Grand Canyon, after I had absorbed its impossible scope for two days and nights, were something like his feelings when he watched his University of Michigan alma mater football team play in the Rose Bowl. Before every such game he would swear not to get emotional or excited. But when the team took the field, urged on by the fighting "Victors" theme song, played by the Michigan band, something changed within him which he could not control. Something irrational, emotional, primal.

That was my feeling as I looked down, my second evening there, on the silent emptiness of Grand Canyon. I already felt that I knew it — from Francis' letters. Its emptiness filled me to overflowing; its silences roused resonating echoes of pride within me. In my varied life, I had lived in 16 different places, had attended probably half as many different schools; my geographical loyalties had become scattered and diluted. But this Canyon was mine. I was a native to this land. Those distances and depths and dioramas spoke my language. Francis expressed it quite well when he said, "Helen, this Canyon is mine by adoption, but it's yours by birth."

I was glad that he had discovered it first, and had grown to love it, before I saw it. From now on, it belonged to us both. Grand Canyon became a mighty factor in our married lives.

With much of America — and Europe also — beckoning us on, there was not time, on this first of my Grand Canyon visits, to explore extensively below the Rim. Perhaps a more practical reason was that I had never done any serious mountain or canyon hiking.

"We'll just take a short foray," Francis suggested, "for a mile or so down the Kaibab Trail — to get the feel and to test our legs."

From the South Kaibab trailhead we started down. I had supposed that the climb back up would be the real test of its difficulties, and that the descent would be simple. That supposition was as far from the truth as the North Rim is from the South. The trail started off with a set of switchbacks and corkscrews that — had I not braced myself — would have pulled me downward so fast that I could have fallen, or turned an ankle, which I sometimes do. It left me breathless.

Francis often has to wrestle with a tendency to hike too fast. I am somewhat the opposite and on this first-ever Grand Canyon hike of mine I found two excellent reasons to take my time.

Almost at once I began to realize how different the Canyon looks when down in it than when viewed from the Rim. Those cold rock walls had become our close companions. They displayed strange patterns and configurations which needed time for study. Also, I needed time to adjust to the steepness of our descent.

Before starting down, Francis had indicated that there would be some gentle slopes along the way, even one or two nearly level stretches. If so, I missed them completely. After a seeming eternity, when the trail did straighten out and ease up a bit, at Cedar Ridge, I sat down under one of the old gnarled trees[1] for which the place is named, and confessed: "I never knew I was such a tenderfoot!"

Then I queried: "Do you think I can make it back up? Is the whole trail this hard?"

After some hesitation Francis answered that latter query.

"Here at Cedar Ridge it is nearly level for a ways. But then it really gets steep. If we can go just a little farther — out to the edge of this clear place — you can see how it looks down below."

We went — I saw. We turned back toward that tree and took another long rest, preparatory to the upward climb. For the first time I really became relaxed enough to begin enjoying the qualities and atmosphere of this world we had penetrated. I was actually *in* Grand Canyon. The complete silence which surrounded us was as expansive as the views. We sat for a long time, not so much to rest, for now I was feeling refreshed, but just to see and feel and absorb. We'd probably have sat even longer but the rays of the sun, which had been steadily arching across the sky, began to strike us with stinging blasts of heat. Rather than move back into the shade, we concluded that we better head on out before that sun turned up its thermostat any higher. Just then we heard a strange noise.

Down along the nearly level part of the trail below, a figure was stumbling toward us. It was a boy, maybe 16 or so. Our canteen of water still lay on the ground beside us. With a pleading look in his eyes he grabbed it and started drinking.

"Wait," yelled Francis. "You may be thirsty but that's the only water between here and the top."

The boy was almost completely dehydrated. When he was able to talk he told us that he and two buddies had started up from the river that morning.

"We didn't know we'd need water," he admitted. When their exhaustion had become complete, they had abandoned their heavy packs. As he was half incoherently telling his story, his two buddies appeared, obviously in even worse shape.

Francis and I held a whispered conference. In our packs, we had one other canteen of water but for the present we kept that fact a secret. When the other boys — about the same age — made it up to our shade, Francis gave each of them two swallows of water, then explained.

"Boys, you're in deep trouble. And so are we. Look at that sun. It's hot, and it's getting hotter. And the trail is getting steeper. We're going to share our water with you, but you're going to have to do a lot of climbing between each swig." For the next couple of hours, the promise of those widely-spaced swallows of water is all that kept the boys going. Francis mentally measured off and calculated the distances; about every thousand feet we'd stop, and the boys would get one swig apiece.

As I brought up the rear, many thoughts raced through my mind. How providential it was that we happened to be on that trail that day when those boys were in dire need of water. What would have happened to them had we not gone on our "little foray?" We had not passed any other individuals on the Kaibab Trail that afternoon. There must be some kind of inner guidance even when we do not know it. We were so thankful we were there when needed.

Francis and I never drank a drop of water on that sunbaked upward climb. I can't remember that I even realized there were any switchbacks. So intent were we on getting those young fellows to the top, we even forgot that the Canyon beauties were still spread all around us. There was probably half a cup of hot precious liquid in the last of our canteens when we approached the final switchback.

"Here, boys, you divide it up." For the first time, Francis relinquished his hold on the water. The boys almost fought over those last few drops.

By now I had faintly come to my senses and realized that I'd made it — a mile-and-a-half down, and a mile-and-a-half back up — on one of the steeper trails in the Canyon. In sweltering weather. I had been initiated. Francis said I'd passed the test. Then he added, "Maybe we can do some more testing sometime. I hope we'll be hiking all these trails a lot."

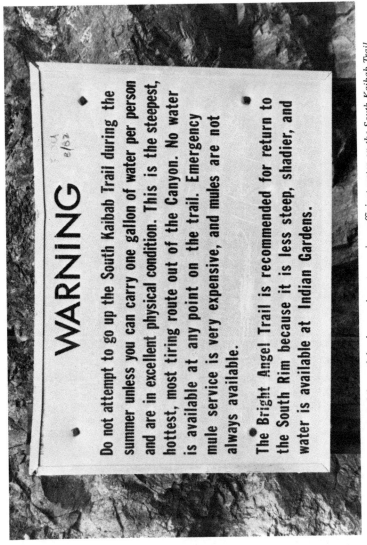

WARNING

Do not attempt to go up the South Kaibab Trail during the summer unless you can carry one gallon of water per person and are in excellent physical condition. This is the steepest, hottest, most tiring route out of the Canyon. No water is available at any point on the trail. Emergency mule service is very expensive, and mules are not always available.

The Bright Angel Trail is recommended for return to the South Rim because it is less steep, shadier, and water is available at Indian Gardens.

A sign warns today's hikers of the dangers in not carrying sufficient water on the South Kaibab Trail.

After we had had some lemonade at the village, and I was completely rested, I hoped so too.

XIII

Grand Canyon Is In Our Blood

by Helen

My first meeting with Francis resulted from a chain of coincidences. Had he and his brother not been persuaded — on their hiking odyssey around the United States — to take the side trip up California's Redwood Highway, we never would have met. (See Chapter 3) If they had been able to shave in the salt water of Arcata Bay at Eureka, they would not have stopped to shave in the tiny stream in front of my home; our paths would never have crossed. A dozen "ifs" on that day resulted in bringing us together.

Another coincidence — a rather insignificant one on another occasion — also changed our lives completely, leading us into our lifelong profession, and helping to bind us even more strongly to the Grand Canyon. In the years of the great depression, as a present, I gave Francis an inexpensive 16mm motion picture camera. That gift turned our lives completely around.

Without benefit of lessons, Francis discovered that he had a natural knack at shooting superior motion pictures, which at the same time told a story. I found that I had a special ability at editing them. Our "home" movies were sought after by service clubs, women's clubs, elementary schools, high schools, and junior colleges in the area where we lived. Almost nightly we were kept busy showing our films, accompanying them with commentary.

"Helen, a bee is buzzing in my bonnet," Francis commented one day. "We can't go on showing films and lecturing every night, for free. We and our calendar would both soon be exhausted. Let's make a full-length color motion picture that we can charge for."

Without realizing what lay ahead, and with almost no knowledge of the then fledgling travel-adventure-lecture business, we were groping toward something that would occupy our lives for 40 years. We were about to make a lifetime profession out of a backyard hobby.

At first, the whole world was our workshop — Lapland (in winter), Finland, England, Holland, Japan, China, the Dutch East Indies, the Philippines, Hawaii. Then, in the war year of 1943, Francis followed a herd of sheep, for 40 days, as their Mexican herder drove them from winter pasture near Phoenix, to the cooler summer range in the mountains of north-central Arizona. The resulting "Sheep, Stars, and Solitude" became the leading lecture film in America, eclipsing everything else that we had done. Seldom again did we go abroad for film production. Western America became our cinematic workshop. And partly because of its strategic location in western America, but more particularly because of its cinematic lure, and our love for it, the Grand Canyon became a principal centerpiece of our filming endeavors.

"Seven Wonders of the West." In that hour-and-a-half long production, Grand Canyon stood at the top.

"Road to Grandeur." In following U.S. 89, America's most scenic highway, from the Canadian Rockies to Arizona's Mexican border, the adjacent national parks, such as Yellowstone, Bryce, Zion, and Grand Canyon, all became grist for our cinematic mill.

"Navajo, A People Between Two Worlds." Grand Canyon National Park adjoins the vast Navajo reservation along its

64

In 1943 Francis filmed a 40-day Arizona sheep trek which terminated 125 miles southeast of Grand Canyon. The success of that motion picture turned the Lines toward the filming of western America, including the Canyon.

western border and was a part of the story. Probably 50 times we visited the Canyon, enroute to or from the reservation.

"This Is Your America" had to include a reference to the Canyon.

"Southwest Story" was centered in southern Utah and the Arizona "strip," including the Kaibab Forest and the North Rim.

"Best of the West" was a resume of our travels in Western America; the film ended with *the* best of all — the Grand Canyon.

We filmed the West, but most of our showings — at travel-adventure lecture series, at universities, museums, libraries, and schools — were in the Midwest and East. When one or both of us would travel from our California home to a series of such engagements, in the autumn and in the spring, we would often stop at Grand Canyon's South Rim for relaxation.

On the many transcontinental flights which we had to make, never once did we sit anywhere except at a window seat. While fellow passengers slept or read, we would watch America's scenery unfolding below. We knew the landscape by heart — almost every road or important landmark west of the Rockies. Even at 30,000 feet aloft, we often made out the suspension bridge over the Colorado River near Phantom Ranch. Or El Tovar. Or the Bright Angel Fault. Or Lake Mead at the Canyon's western end, or Lake Powell (after Glen Canyon Dam was finished) at its eastern extremity. At 30,000 feet the details disappeared and blended into a mightly panorama of color and master design.

In our earliest visits to Grand Canyon's North or South Rims, we always camped out. Francis' first visit to the North Rim was before there was a lodge, or any formal visitor accommodations there. In later years we began using the cabins, which afforded better shelter for our photographic equipment, and gave us better lighting for reading and writing at night. On one special occasion we stayed in the Presidential Suite of El Tovar Lodge, but camps and campfires or rustic housekeeping cabins suited our needs much better.

Often we have been asked, "How many times have you visited Grand Canyon?" Our answer has to be,

"Not enough."

In the filming of <u>Road to Grandeur</u>, Francis and Helen journeyed often to the national parks along the route, including Grand Canyon.

Francis and Helen's daughter Adrienne had her first view of Grand Canyon on one of her parents' many visits there.

The Canyon is in our blood. New experiences are there awaiting us. There is still so much to see. We have scarcely scratched the surface. And the surface is so large . . .

XIV

Coasting Canyonward

1944-'45

We probably should not have been surprised at the strange circumstances which occurred when we were camped on Grand Canyon's North Rim, one of the most remote spots in America.

Unusual circumstances had played a large role in the methods by which we were able to reach that spot. One of the finest achievements of our professional motion picture filming career unfolded while we were camped there.

But none of these circumstances prepared us for what was to follow.

The spot was Cape Royal, reached by an interesting and narrow winding road through the Kaibab Forest 20 miles southeast of the deserted lodge on Grand Canyon's North Rim.

The time was August, in the war year of 1945.

Cape Royal was not only 20 miles from the empty lodge, it was 60 miles from the nearest base of accessible supplies at the equally remote crossroads of Jacob Lake to the north. It was many hundreds of miles from any major city.

The view from Cape Royal — one of the choice vistas which can be had of Grand Canyon — was worth all the trials

Francis and Helen had often looked across at Cape Royal from the South Rim (it is at the tip of the flat plateau as Helen films it) but had never visited it until 1945.

Helen surveys the Canyon from the North Rim.

which we had encountered to get there.

Traveling by automobile in the gas-starved war years of 1944 and 1945 was an experience in ingenuity and patience. One day I burst into the living room of our home which straddled the Pasadena-Eagle Rock city limits in Southern California.

"Helen," I announced excitedly to her. "I've just been over talking with the Buffs. They drove to the North Rim country and they said they *coasted* a quarter of the way, to save gas. If they can do it, so can we."

From that minute on, we started hoarding our gas ration coupons and in the early summer of 1944, accompanied by our seven-and-a-half-year-old daughter Adrienne, we started out for Mt. Carmel, Utah, which would be the base for our film work in the North Rim Grand Canyon area. We would share artist Maynard Dixon's rustic home.

By actual odometer measurement, we coasted 156 miles of the total 500 mile distance — with only one critical episode.

Before exiting from California, Helen had taken the wheel as we started down the long grade toward Stateline, on the Nevada border, heading toward the (at that time) small gambling town of Las Vegas. Our car, in neutral, with the motor off, picked up enormous speed. Faster. Then even faster. Luckily we were the only vehicle traveling in either direction; gas rationing had turned the wartime highways almost into ghost lanes.

Helen, clutching the wheel, attempted to brake the car, but without results.

Faster yet.

In the distance, with no notice at all, appeared a major turn in the highway, where our route veered leftward toward Vegas. The road straight ahead — where that went we did not know.

"I can't make it," cried Helen. "What shall I do?"

"Don't try it." My voice was choked as I yelled to her. "Keep going straight."

That coast was the longest of our trip. There were no other side roads in that isolated desert. Without benefit of gas, when the car finally came to a stop, we were well on our way to Searchlight, Nevada, a semi-ghost town, which made a suitable spot for camping out over night.

We still had a gas coupon or so in our ration book when we

74

pulled into Maynard Dixon's place in the hamlet of Mt. Carmel, close to the Arizona-Utah border. Now we could give our car a long rest, as we would use other means, for a while, to get where we needed to go. Several times we rode with Tom Blackburn, who had a roadside gem shop behind his house in Mt. Carmel, and who made distant forays into remote areas above Grand Canyon, seeking rare specimens of rocks. We often received lifts from the kind Mormon cowboys and ranchers. And occasionally we rode in Maynard Dixon's station wagon as he sought out scenes, that only an artist would know about, to put on canvas. He had his own gas supply; in tagging along with him we not only filmed scenic wonders on our own, but made a reel or so of film catching this man at his painting — a man who, after his death two years later, would rank among the greatest of western artists. His canvases are now rare treasures. If we had had a big supply of gas coupons, we might possibly have traded him for one or two of those paintings which he made as we filmed.

On several occasions we journeyed with two government trappers — a husband-and-wife team — as they inspected their trap lines in remote regions of the Kaibab National Forest above North Rim. The only space available for us and our camera equipment was in the back of their pickup truck, filled with coyote traps and manure. But on that journey we received an introduction to the Kaibab country that could have been obtained in no other way.

I had first traveled to the Grand Canyon's North Rim, and this Kaibab Forest country, twenty years before, on Independence Day — July 4 — 1925. With my parents and brother, we had been roughing it by car through the West, and were headed to Bryce Canyon from Zion National Park. The great highway tunnel which today affords easy access between these parks did not exist then.

We backtracked toward Hurricane, then made an enormous swing through an isolated area in the Arizona "strip" (the region north of the Grand Canyon) to Fredonia, before heading north to Bryce.

The climb from the Zion area up to the highlands had been wicked, and it dumped us onto a narrow dirt road which carried

75

us through wild country until darkness took over, and we made camp in the junipers with a roaring fire. Next day, at Pipe Spring, had come the first chance to fill up with water, and at Fredonia, population 50, the first chance for gas.

Bryce lay to the north, but the Grand Canyon's North Rim had lured us southward. More bad roads. Rain. Then the Kaibab Forest, and fine open meadows. Deer! My brother and I had started counting. By the time we were ready to pitch camp near the Canyon's Rim we had counted 146 Kaibab deer. Next day we counted 298 more. A ranger told us that the Kaibab deer were becoming so numerous that they were destroying the forest growth, which was their natural food. A Flagstaff cowboy, George McCormick, aided by Zane Grey, with many Indians and cowboys, had tried to drive some of the deer down the trails and over to the South Rim. The effort was a failure.

Rain had been falling, so the ranger told us,[1] for five days. But the moment of sunset on that first visit of mine had brought clearing skies. A curtain of haze lifted, the golden sun became a great spotlight, and I had my first perfect view of the Canyon from the North Rim. There was no North Rim Lodge in those days; few visitors besides ourselves were there. We and the deer shared the Rim and the Kaibab Forest almost all to ourselves.

I thought about that first visit of mine to this area — and recounted details of it to Helen — as she and I rode in the back of the government trappers' truck along the trails and through the trees and meadows of the Kaibab Forest. These trappers were being paid by the government to destroy the predators in the region, yet this was the very thing that had resulted in the forest's overpopulation of deer in the year of my first visit here — 1925. The deer population had grown from 4000 in the early 1900s, to an estimated 100,000 in 1924-25 — the critical years. Nature, in the form of coyotes and mountain lions, had once maintained a proper balance.

With predators gone, the abnormal populations of deer, in search of sustenance to avoid starvation, began to destroy the forests. The living inner bark of the pine tree is their food. Government policy encouraged hunting to thin the herds but, contrary to the natural process, hunters usually shoot the finest, healthiest deer, while the predators nearly always caught and ate the weaker ones. Thus the quality of the herds was lowered. It was a long time before government policy changed, and nature was allowed to take command again.

Much as Helen and I hated to see the coyotes trapped, we none-the-less took every advantage of our rides with the trappers. There were a dozen opportunities a day to film the deer — in herds, in pairs, or singly, grazing in unconcern, or watching us intently, or bouncing with the grace of ballet dancers through the trees.

We became acquainted with — and made many motion picture studies of — the Kaibab squirrels as well, which are delightful residents there.

This Kaibab Forest and Plateau are cut off, by the Canyon, from its surroundings. The Kaibab squirrel on the North Rim, and its cousin, the Abert squirrel on the South, are doubtless descended from common ancestors. But the Canyon has separated them for such a long time that they have developed independently. The North Rim's Kaibab creature is white-tailed and black-bellied; its South Rim cousin is grey-tailed and white-bellied. Both have tufted ears in winter. The Kaibab squirrel is found nowhere else in the world except Grand Canyon's North Rim.

This beautiful creature had one characteristic common to other squirrels we've known — it liked peaches. As we were camping deep in the forest, one of them pilfered a peach out of the trappers' food supply. It started for a tree and we started for our movie camera. That squirrel actually made it up to the middle branches of a ponderosa pine, carrying the peach in its mouth. We have proof of it on film. Twice it dropped the prize, but did not give up. In haughty grandeur it consumed the peach — as we watched and filmed.

In this North Rim country, we were enticed once by the lure of Point Sublime, where our camping spot had an immensity of Canyon view which swept around much of the horizon.

Once we went beyond the Kaibab Forest, down to House Rock Valley, to film the buffalo that were there, enclosed in an enormous grazing region by the natural barriers of the Colorado River, the Vermillion Cliffs, and the Kaibab Plateau. Hunting up the game warden, Slim Latham, we bumped for 15 miles out over wild "buffalo" land, twice hanging up briefly on rocks. The reward was a herd of nearly 200 buffalo.

The North Rim area and its Kaibab Forest, in its natural isolation, became a favorite region for us.

Francis films some of the 200 buffalo which roamed in House Rock Valley, adjacent to Kaibab Forest and the Colorado River.

XV

North Rim Magic

1945

Storing our car in southern Utah, we commuted home by bus several times to get more camera supplies and develop our film.

"You people deserve more gasoline," the chairman of our gas rationing board told me on one of these commuter trips back to California. It was now mid 1945. "We've been hearing about your work. You are doing the nation a great service."

Word had come to him from several cities across America where I had lectured with our motion pictures during the winter.[1]

"You are taking America to them, so they don't have to use gas to go out and see it for themselves," the chairman continued.

Some extra gas, to us, was more life-sustaining than a blood transfusion to a dying man. I followed the chairman's lead by excitedly explaining that I had also shown our films, as a free public service, to groups of draftees and servicemen.

"We're going to issue you a "C" ration book." The chairman shook my hand warmly as he intoned those sacred words.

Journeying by bus back to the North Rim country, with new

"THE MAN WHO HAS PRODUCED THE PERFECT FILM."

—James B. Pond, Editor
Program Magazine.

FRANCIS R. LINE

SIX LECTURE QUALIFICATIONS . . .
AN INTRODUCTION BY "QUOTES"

1. "One of the world's best color photographers."
—George Pierrot, Director,
World Adventure Series, Detroit.

2. "Excellence of narration."
—Melville Grosvenor, National Geographic
Society, Washington, D.C.

3. "A vital sense of humor. An outstanding platform personality."
—Hazel L. Muller, Program Director,
American Museum of Natural History,
New York.

4. "A splendid lecture. A careful and painstaking treatment of material."
—Dr. Paul H. Sheats, Educational Director,
The Town Hall, New York.

5. "The story you told was of Epical proportions, in the true sense of the word."
—Dr. Julius Bloom, Director,
The Brooklyn Institute.

6. "When beauty of pictures can be combined with a running commentary packed with authoritative facts, the program is unbeatable."
—Seattle Post-Intelligencer.

Francis took films of western America across the United States on regular lecture tours. This was the cover of one of his brochures.

ration books in our possession, we took our car out of mothballs, realizing that we would not have to coast quite so much — at least in the more dangerous places. But we still had to conserve fuel in every way possible; a "C" book was no magic carpet.

Featured occasionally in our film, in addition to our daughter Adrienne, were Victor and Gail, Tom Blackburn's grandchildren who lived with Tom and his wife. Victor was ten, Gail eight, and Adrienne nearly nine. For a week, we and the three youngsters had been traveling in remote areas of the North Rim country. In far away Europe, Germany had fallen. The war in the Pacific was climaxing; gas was harder to come by than ever.

Coffee and sugar were rationed, too. We used almost none of either. Once, when our gas coupons were nearly exhausted, we effected a trade at the home of a lonely rancher. As a cattle producer, he had all the gas he wanted but was completely out of sugar and coffee. With the tank of gas from that trade we drove first down to North Rim Lodge. It was closed for the duration. But it was far from deserted. Some half a hundred Kaibab deer had taken possession.

"Look, mama, there are six deer on the porch," came Adrienne's excited cry.

"Look there. That one's peeking in the window." This from Victor, equally excited.

There were deer on the sidewalks and paths, and six or eight grazing in a small meadow close by. Beyond that were more than we could count. Going carefully around to the front of the deserted lodge, we saw two of the graceful creatures apparently taking in the Canyon view.

Cape Royal lay 20 miles east and south — nearly two gallons of gas, roundtrip. We decided to make it. That two gallons was the most productive that any car of ours has ever consumed. Cape Royal provided us with front row balcony seats overlooking a natural stage play which, although in its millionth plus year of continuous performance, was adding new acts, and fresh changes of sets and scenes, every hour. As near to the point as we could get we established camp, as I jokingly said, "for the duration."

Just ahead was Wotan's Throne, probably once a part of

83

Gail, Adrienne, and Victor absorb the view from Cape Royal.

Victor makes friends with a Kaibab Forest fawn.

Cape Royal but now an isolated island — a gigantic rock throne dominating the entire landscape. Its great walls are chameleon in character, as they change color with the rising sun as it turns its orange spotlight on it; and again at evening as the sky and sun become one and their bright red colors dye Wotan to match their own brilliance. It is pure breathtaking splendor — a throne fit for a king!

Now it was sunset time. Helen with her Leica, I with the movie camera, were methodically filming the final act of this day's stage drama, just before the curtain was due to drop. Through the camera finder I suddenly saw a flash of unrehearsed action.

"Look," I called to Helen. The youngsters said it was not a call, but a frantic yell. "Look, there's a hummingbird right in my lens."

Between camera and sunset-draped Wotan's Throne was a thistle plant festooned with a score of delicate blossoms. That is what I was filming. But, as though one of those blossoms had magically grown wings and come alive, a nectar-seeking hummingbird was occupying the center stage. It had come for its ambrosial nightcap. That is what I was shouting about.

The vast Canyon in mysterious shadows.

Wotan's Throne, in sunset splendor, throbbing with reckless splashes of evening sunlight.

A floral bouquet fit for heavenly kings and queens.

And a tiny hummingbird, lord of it all.

This, in a single shot! Photographers sometimes get unearned rewards.

Francis is out at dawn to film the hummingbird (marked by arrow) with his telephoto lens.

XVI

Cape Royal Celebration

We needn't have been frantic about our filming. The hummingbird worked about the thistle plant until dark.

And it was there again at dawn. I was set with my camera while the whole Canyon was still swallowed in blackness, so I even beat the hummingbird to its work. "The early bird catches the worm," Helen joked.

That hummer became the focal point of our filming for three days and nights. We caught it against a background of the Canyon in sunrise and sunset light, subdued by clouds, one morning wrapped in a gentle fog, once even under a veil of rain. Then — a chromatic climax — the colorful hummingbird against a flaming red before-dusk Canyon, with a double rainbow arching the entire scene.

The month was wearing on — August 14, 1945. Too emotionally worn out with it all — physically tired also — I didn't sleep too well that night, and switched on the car radio in the wee hours. The hummingbird sequence had been for us a personal climax in our careers as professional motion picture photographers. What I heard on the radio at 2 or 3 o'clock that

89

morning was a climax for the entire world. I uttered a shout, more frenzied than had come at first view of the hummingbird. It awoke Helen and the kids. They crowded into the car — and all bent to listen.

"Japan has surrendered. The war is over," I shouted. The news came to us in one of America's most remote spots. We were completely, unutterably alone. But at that moment the whole world seemed very close — and dear. Peace! We said some prayers of thanks that early morning.

I never slept at all, and never took my ear from the radio. Toward dawn another flash. Strange — yet really perhaps not so strange, after all — that this second news flash should be the first vital one following the surrender bulletin. Shaking Helen awake, I relayed to her the radio bulletin: "Gas rationing is ended."

Helen prepared a hurry-up breakfast. I filmed several more shots of the hummingbird but can't even remember whether the sky was cloudy or clear. On the way to the nearest phone — 60 miles distant, at Jacob Lake, just a wide place in the forest — we held a Council of Peace.

For years we'd had almost no gas. Our professional film work had suffered considerably. We needed other scenes of the Southwest to complete our film story of this vast area of which the Grand Canyon was the centerpiece. What better time than now.

Yes, Grandma and Grandpa Blackburn said, it would be perfectly agreeable for Gail and Victor to be gone a while if we wished to take them with us on our journey.

It chagrined me that there were still a few unused gas coupons in our ration book. But without need of them we filled the tank, turned our car — not back to Mt. Carmel — but east and south toward Cameron and Flagstaff, and started out on the strangest week of touring we had ever had, or probably will ever experience again.

Flagstaff. No room at the Inn. Or at the tourist camps either. Holbrook the same. And Winslow. And Gallup, New Mexico.

Highway 66, as we traveled by night, was almost one continuous makeshift camping spot and row of campfires. Tens of thousands of gas-hungry and vacation-starved citizens of California and Arizona were celebrating America's victory by taking to

90

the road. Highways that for a year had seen only a handful of cars a day — no tourists whatsoever — suddenly became thoroughfares of commerce. A thousand campfires of an army bivouacked in war might have produced a sight such as we saw between Flagstaff and Albuquerque. But these were campfires of peace. Americans seeking release from the emotional strain of war. An emotional binge. A Niagara of travelers flooding Highway 66. A thousand campfires — creating a strange path of light across western America. Someone flying above in an airplane might have thought that the desert was on fire.

For a solid week we were never able to find lodging in a hotel, motel, or regular campground. The banks of impromptu night campfires lining the highway — America's "Main Street" — was one of the strangest sights, in its way, that we had ever seen.

Helen and I like to camp out. But that week was seven days of nearly continuous storm! Albuquerque — rain, and no place to stay. We spent most of the night — five of us — sleeping in our five-passenger car.

Santa Fe. Somewhat the same. Since it rained but little, Helen and I found places to stretch out on the ground. The three youngsters did quite well in the car.

The message which the raindrops and the overflowing campgrounds — and auto courts — was drumming into us was beginning to take effect on our planning patterns. We must abandon tourist centers, get as far removed from Highway 66 as our car could take us, and pray for clear skies.

Arizona's White Mountains. That area was remote, and we had business there. Two years before I'd made a film — SHEEP, STARS, AND SOLITUDE — following a herd of sheep on a wilderness trek from Arizona's Salt River Valley up over the Mogollon Rim. I had shown the film twice on the National Geographic's lecture course at Constitution Hall in Washington and they had asked me to repeat the trek, to do an article and stills for their magazine. This second journey — to be taken next year — would continue even farther — from the Mogollon into the White Mountains. To get some acquaintance with the area now would help.

So, early on a Sunday morning, we nosed our car south

toward Socorro, then turned due west over one of the remote roads in the state.

Pie Town stood out in isolated splendor on the map. But unless we had driven slowly, and with sharp attention, we might have missed it altogether — two eating places and a filling station.

"Five pieces of apple pie," we said to the woman behind the eating place counter.

"Don't have any pie," she explained. "Not enough customers to keep it fresh."

Here was the first solid evidence, since leaving North Rim, that we had escaped the Highway 66 influence — or at least were ahead of the sudden postwar tourist flood.

With high hopes in our hearts we went on to Springerville — just across the state line in Arizona — for the night.

We had never been to Springerville on a weekend. No doubt, during the week, people live there. But not on Sunday. At least, not one person was visible as we drove around the few streets which held its clusters of houses and stores together. Not one.

This didn't really matter. The one point of interest, to us, was as visible as the Vishnu Temple rising in isolated splendor in the Grand Canyon which we had so recently left. The large white wooden Cattlemen's Hotel had a light inside. Two whole floors of warm rooms. Bathtubs. Showers.

The lank western-dressed cowboy-clerk behind the counter gave me a patronizing smile.

"We got no rooms vacant, pardner," he drawled in a Texas accent. "Sorry. Our rooms are all took on a monthly basis. Ranchers. They use 'em every so often. But they're all rented up. Sorry."

No pie in Pie Town. No vacancies in a two-story hotel in a town where no one seemed to be living.

At least it wasn't raining.

Helen was mad — not angry, but mad.

"I don't care if it's raining or not," was her ultimatum when I went back out to the car with my message of despair. "I need a bath; we all do. Why aren't there any vacant rooms?" She and I went back into the hotel together.

The cowboy-clerk was firm. "I told you — all our spare rooms are leased by the month."

Helen kept talking. Her description of our woes might be making an impression. The clerk began shifting his weight from one foot to the other. Maybe a good sign.

Just then, Adrienne and Victor and Gail came in from the car outside. They were sleepy — and showed it. They were dirty — and looked it. They were hungry — and said so.

"Can't we stay here?" our daughter Adrienne asked, with weariness in her voice. "This place is nice. It's warm in here. Why can't we stay?"

My pleas had had no more effect than a cow horse's tail trying to whisk away flies. Helen's vivid rhetoric had maybe been as though the mare had found a barbed wire fence, and started rubbing and scratching against it.

When the kids appeared — hungry, dirty, tired — and all completely unrehearsed — well, it was like the horse had found a pool of soft dust and could roll in it forever, and kick its legs in the air with glee.

"Look," said the man behind the desk — now more clerk than cowboy. "These ranchers rent those rooms. But some of them's not used much. Jed don't come in hardly ever, on Sunday nights. Probably he'd never know it if I let you have his room."

Five minutes later we were washing, showering, bathing — even rolling on the massive soft bed, almost like Jed's horse might have rolled in some soft pool of dust in the pasture. There were no flies on us. We went down to eat.

"Oh, we don't serve no meals," said our benefactor behind the desk. "Sometimes breakfasts on weekdays. But never anything Sundays."

We had driven all around Springerville; everything was closed — we knew that.

But a small cafe — a sort of hamburger place around the corner and down the next street — we might possibly have some luck there, said the clerk.

"This is Sunday, you know," he cautioned. "But maybe."

We determined to try.

XVII

Hospitality, Western Style

A small light was burning in a rear room of the hamburger place. It was closed.

"Look, mom, there's a man in there." Adrienne, as well as Victor and Gail, had their noses pressed to the window, hands shielding their eyes — peering in.

The front room of the cafe was rather large — neatly arranged with tables and chairs, a large record player against the rear wall, and the serving counter connecting with the rear room, which must have been the kitchen. A light in the record player cast a yellowish glow around the main room. The rear room had its own light — and a man moving about.

I knocked hard on the glass pane of one of the double doors. Results, zero.

I rattled the door vigorously.

"He heard us," announced Victor. "He looked up." Still zero results.

Grabbing the handles of both doors firmly, I shook and rattled them until Helen made me stop.

Results, 100%.

At least, nearly so. The man switched on a light in the front room, came up to the doors, unlocked and opened them, and explained with more courtesy than might have been expected, "We're closed."

The Cattlemen's Hotel experience had made us experts. In all seriousness, we would hardly ever do what we had been doing here in Springerville, but a week such as we had gone through might even have made a beggar out of a king.

As the man had switched on the light and come toward the doors through the front room, the sight of three pairs of childish eyes, glued on him through the window — maybe that had said to him all that was needed.

In a few minutes we were all seated inside at a large table and the man was heating soup and cooking hamburgers in the rear room.

He had forgotten to relock the front doors. From out on the street, a man tried the door, found it open, and came in. This was the first person — other than our hotel and cafe benefactors — that we had seen in Springerville.

"Place was closed an hour ago," said the Stranger. "Glad you're open. I'll have a hamburger and some coffee."

"We're still closed," said the man preparing our food.

Springerville, we were finding, was a place of compassionate people. With no further words, the cafe man — whether he was proprietor, cook, waiter, cashier, or all four, we never knew — was putting another hamburger on to fry.

The Stranger had taken a seat at a table near the center of the large room. We were at one side. Victor, always restless and curious, wandered up to the lighted record player, read the list of recordings, then asked of me, "Can I have a nickel? They've got a good record in there."

I suppose I'm the only person in western America who has never put a nickel — or any other coin — in the slot of a record player to hear canned music. I don't like their artificial clatter. I'd put in money to stop them — but never to set them going. It's one of my peculiarities. I confess it but won't attempt to explain it. I could say that it had been a hard week, and a trying day, but that was not the reason. To Victor's request I simply said "No."

The Stranger was obviously listening. None of us had been

served yet, and there was nothing else to do. He reached into his pocket, fumbled for a coin.

"Here, kid," he motioned to Victor. "Let's hear your tune."

The music was still blaring when our food came but this was once when I didn't let it interfere with my appetite. I was not even too embarrassed over the episode of the nickel.

After too long, the music ceased.

The Stranger at his table, we at ours, were eating — hungrily, silently, earnestly. He finished before we did, but asked for some more coffee.

"First time I've been back here in 45 years," he announced to no one in particular. "Used to work cattle down this way. Had some great times here. Haven't been back in 45 years."

I was glad he had spoken. Secretly I had been concerned that this might have been the absentee Jed, whose room we were occupying at the hotel. Relieved, I said,

"So you worked cattle? My wife's father — most of her relatives — were cattlemen. Down near Globe and Superior — that area. Maybe you've heard of them. Gibsons."

"Gibson?" The Stranger was bypassing me, speaking directly to Helen. "You mean you're a Gibson? Not related to Charlie Gibson by any chance?"

"He's my uncle," said Helen.

The Stranger became a stranger no longer. We found his name was Jack. Even the cook, proprietor, waiter and cashier came in to listen as Jack recounted episodes of early Springerville days when he and Charlie Gibson used to work together on ranches in this region.

Our conversation was taking place across the customerless cavern of the unfilled room. We had to raise our voices a bit to be heard. Jack finished his refill of coffee, looked across at Helen with a hesitant expression, then motioned with his arm and index finger.

"Come here," he almost whispered. Helen answered his look, glanced at me questioningly, then the both of us went over to his table.

Jack was speaking so low now that we had to bend close to hear.

"Do you know about Charlie Gibson and the cattle rustler?" he asked.

We didn't.

"Charlie had to use his gun." explained Jack. "He was riding out toward the creek when he saw the widow who lives near there driving her cattle along toward a corral. A man on horseback suddenly appeared out of nowhere, and cut some of the cattle out.

"That's when Charlie came up. 'Leave that widow's cattle alone,' he yelled.

"The man didn't pay a bit of attention.

"I'm warning you," yelled Charlie.

"The man reached for his gun but Charlie reached for his faster and sent a bullet singing through the air. The last he saw of the rustler, he was hell-bent for Texas. Don't know if the bullet hit him or not.

"The widow wasn't about to keep a story like that to herself. Charlie was soon quite a hero."

* * * * *

In the first beds we'd occupied for a week, we caught up on a lot of sleep that night. Not even the prospect that Jed might check into his room — or dreams of cattle rustlers — kept us awake.

98

XVIII

Say Uncle!

Next morning it was raining. Enroute back to Grand Canyon, we headed for Payson, home of a noted rodeo.

Payson's affair is not like the ones at Pendleton or at Bozeman, where the riders are mainly professionals who travel the circuit. These Payson riders — at least the majority of them — are genuine cowhands vying with one another in saddle and roping skills. It is for real. We had long wanted to film the event. Now we found ourselves in Payson at just the right time. By laying over one day we could film the rodeo, if the rain would stop. All five of us showed our excitement as we went into the town's hotel for a room.

"Got a reservation?" asked the man in charge.

"Do we need one?"

"Need one? Hell, our rooms are reserved a year ahead at rodeo time."

If it wasn't ration-weary travelers letting off steam after years of war, it was backwoods cowboys, in off the range for the rodeo, crowding the town until it was ready to split open. As the rain intensified Helen declared: "I don't think I can sleep another night — five in a car.''

Until suppertime we searched for a place to stay. The town was so crowded with cowboys and sightseers that it seemed like a madhouse.

After supper, almost aimlessly, we continued searching. At about 8 o'clock, in a heavy, increasing downpour, we headed north out of town, through the pines — why, none of us really knew. No motels. No campgrounds. Not even any place to keep dry. I swung into a rancher's gateway to turn around. The drive was at the back of the old ranch house, and a light shown from inside.

''That's a big house. Maybe they'd put us up.'' By her tone, I could see that Helen had really meant that one more night in the car was not for her.

I knocked at the back door. ''Who is it?'' came a woman's voice.

Luckily the rain was making too much noise for her to hear me, because my explanation wasn't very convincing. How do you explain to a woman, through a locked door, that you want to spend the night in her house?

Helen had come up, and she joined my shouts. The woman inside — bless her soul for a courageous individual — unlocked and opened the door. The kids had tagged behind Helen. All five of us crowded into the kitchen.

Three weeks before, that woman's husband had died. In the nighttime emptiness of the big old ranch house, with the rain tattooing a dirge of loneliness against every window pane, the woman almost took us into her arms in welcome.

Yes, there was a bed for Helen and me. And she could fix a place somewhere for the children.

''This is real Arizona hospitality,'' beamed Helen in thanks. ''I was born in Arizona — on a ranch, too, and I know.''

''You were born here? Where?,'' our benefactor wanted to know.

''Globe,'' said Helen.

''Globe? Why, that's our county seat.''

This was a fact, although we hadn't realized it. Arizona's counties are large; Globe was nearly a hundred miles away, over a wicked dirt road.

"Yes," Helen continued, "I moved away from Globe when I was a little girl, but I still have relatives there. My uncle, Mark Hicks, has a large ranch near there."

"Mark Hicks?"

Helen could not have spoken a more magic name if she had entoned the title for God.

"Mark Hicks! Why, he's my supervisor. Finest man in Gila County. Mark Hicks is your uncle? I just can't believe it."

Although we had had a rush-up supper in a jammed cafe in Payson, we were — at this dear lady's insistence — soon downing sandwiches and milk at her kitchen table. As we prepared for bed, she gave Helen a hug and tears came to her eyes. "I just can't believe it!" she almost sang.

We slept in ranch-ready beds. Next morning we had a true ranch breakfast as our hostess and Helen talked Arizona until a beam of morning sun sprinkled into the windows through the pines, and we realized the rain had ceased.

Apparently we had done this gracious widow of Payson a real favor by staying with her and easing the pain of her loneliness. But she had done us a greater one.

Almost forgetting the nights we had spent in the car without sleep, we filmed the rodeo that day and headed back to the North Rim. The hummingbird, bless its soul, was still guarding its royal domain. As I filmed anew, Helen wrote a long letter to her Uncle Mark — Supervisor Mark Hicks, if you please — asking him to be certain, on his next trip up to Payson, to stop in and meet one of his great admirers, the widow who had taken us in out of the rain and turned our discomfort into sunshine.

Twice more, before winter completely seized North Rim in its frozen grip, we returned to Cape Royal from our home in California. The thistle blooms had metamorphosed into fluffy seed-laden delicate globes, which floated out over the Canyon as they hitchhiked with the wind. On our last visit, some snow was falling. The hummingbird was still there.

On their return to Cape Royal, Francis and Helen stopped to give Gail and Victor their first view of the South Rim. The tip of Cape Royal is dimly visible, in the distance, between them.

Adrienne and Victor are glad to be back at Cape Royal and the hummingbird.

XIX

By Jeep to Toroweap
by Helen

1955

Parts of Grand Canyon are in the sphere of the Navajo Nation; for nearly 70 miles, their reservation's western boundary borders Grand Canyon National Park. During two years while producing a documentary film on the land of the Navajo, we traveled by four-wheel-drive Jeep over more than ten thousand miles of their land, which is as large as the combined states of Massachusetts, Connecticut, Rhode Island, and Vermont.

Possessing a Jeep — or any four-wheel-drive vehicle which frees one of the need to stick to main roads — can change one's life. That was the case with us, in the years from 1954 to '56.

On our Jeep trips to and from California, in studying our map we often noticed the thin line of a road leading south from St. George, Utah, to Toroweap Point on the North Rim of Grand Canyon.

Toroweap is one place to dream about. And we had been doing just that, for nearly ten years. We knew that it was one of the Canyon's most cherished viewpoints. But we also knew that it was one of the most isolated — most difficult to reach.

Edwin Corle's 1946 book, LISTEN, BRIGHT ANGEL, had

By Jeep, the Lines journeyed to what is sometimes called "the Grand Canyon of the Upper Colorado," above Moab, Utah.

106

first whetted our appetites for Toroweap. He wrote: "Here is something to take your breath away, literally and figuratively. There is no describing Toroweap Point. With that I'm sure any visitor will agree. Take a good look."[1]

Now that we had a Jeep, we decided to take such a look. But which way to go? There were two routes into this remote section of the Canyon — one by way of Fredonia and Pipe Spring, Arizona, the other from St. George, Utah. Since Corle's book had first stimulated our interest in Toroweap, and since he had described the route out of Pipe Spring as "a road in name only" we decided not to go from there.

It was a wise decision. We *came back out* that way and discovered that — in addition to finding a road in name only — we encountered 12 — we counted them — 12 wire gates strung across our route. Corle hadn't mentioned these; perhaps they had been added since his book was written. One of us would jump out, get the gate unfastened and opened, let the other drive through, then fasten the gate again. "Gate" is a misnomer. They were mainly crude wire barriers strung across our path. Twice it took both of us, tugging and lifting, to get them unfastened.

After we had negotiated an even dozen of these barriers I started singing a song that I remembered, "Twelve Gates to the City."

If we had gone in that way, all these gates, and the fact that we wouldn't have known what was coming next, might have discouraged us. Luckily, we took the other route, which provided interesting adventures of its own.

Heading south from St. George, within six or eight miles we left Utah and entered the Arizona "strip," that isolated section which is completely cut off from the rest of the state by the Grand Canyon's impassable gorge.

Our route, on the map we were following, was peppered with names — Wolf Hole Mountain, Mustang Knoll, Sullivan Draw, Diamond Butte. Francis was too busy trying to steer around and avoid the knolls and buttes and bumps in the road to enjoy the larger ones, shown on the map. This was a little-used, lonesome road. Or rather, lonesome *roads*. At one place, three unmarked possible routes offered us a multiple choice.

Eeny, meeny, miney, mo.

We hoped that we had chosen correctly. But not being sure — in a lonely land — brings feelings of apprehension. The appearance of what looked like ranch buildings far ahead was the most welcome sight since entering the strip.

Ranch house it was. No one was about. We knocked at the door. No response. We went out toward the barn. A middle-aged woman, browned from the wind and sun, emerged from the structure and saw us. We thought she might be frightened at the sight of strangers. But instead of fright there was surprising warmth in her greeting. We were soon introducing ourselves to — and becoming acquainted with — Mattie Kent — Mrs. William A. Kent of Tuweep, Arizona.

"Tuweep — oh, that's just short for Toroweap," she explained, in answer to one of the flood of questions which we unloosed on her.

"It's still quite a ways down to the Point. But, yes, you're on the right road." Between answers to our questions she invited us up to the house.

"It's lonesome here now. My husband had to go to Las Vegas for some machinery parts."

We learned that they usually went into St. George for regular supplies. Now, for several days, she would be alone — in charge of the ranch, milking the cows and doing the chores.

We found that they had a son, Hugh Kent, living in Southern California and we promised to phone him when we returned home. We made another pleasant discovery. Mattie Kent served meals to the occasional outsiders who came this way.

"When we come back out, we'll surely stop," we assured her.

As we drove on we were both quiet. Meeting Mrs. Kent had been our only human contact since leaving St. George. We thought about the lonely life of this couple, living on the edge of time — Grand Canyon time.

Our excitement returned as the great rocks of the Toroweap Rim became visible. We parked the Jeep and scrambled over rough ground to stand on the very edge.

Here was the most precipitous drop that we had ever seen in Grand Canyon. Far below, the architect of all this wonder — the Colorado River — was flowing in the rock-ribbed channel of its narrow gorge. In the more familiar parts of the Canyon, such as the Bright Angel area, that gorge gives way to the ten-mile wide — or more — expanse of the upper walls. Here at Toroweap the narrow walls of the gorge came straight up to meet our eyes. We looked almost straight down.

Corle was certainly right in his description: "One of the most stunning spots in the world. You'll be more than a mile (6000 ft.) above the Colorado River, the walls of the inner gorge of the Grand Canyon are closer here than at any point farther east; the entire experience is one that you cannot believe is possible . . . If you've seen all the other points of the Grand Canyon, the devil and the angel have one more knockout punch to throw at you, and this is it!"[2]

As we peered into the deep Canyon we felt it was exactly as Corle described it. *This was it!* The depth, the colors, the roughness, the grandeur. Standing here alone, with the silence all around us, and in us, we felt a great calm of our spirits. The intangibles of this world are perhaps the most real things, at least they are the things which give life its zest and excitement!

A lonesome point in time, for us too. The sun was casting long shadows, purpling the cliffs; we thought that some Beethoven music would fit such a scene. It was a new experience in depth and silence as we stood and waited until the sun was lost to view as the earth turned on its axis. As the earth turns we are no longer the same — we change just as the earth changes on its journey.

Night, with its starry heaven, clothed us in a subtle softness. We realized we had not eaten since early morning. Gathering a few sticks of dry greasewood (Toroweap is the Paiute Indian word for "Greaswood Valley") we built a small fire and opened a can of beans, which we hurriedly heated in our Dutch oven. We put our bread on top to heat while we sliced some cheese. A small tin can held water, and when it was steaming we put some special vegetable-mineral seasoning into it. It made a delicious broth, assuring us of a good night's sleep. A can of pears made a refreshing dessert.

The moon came over the horizon, and added to the mystery of the sky and the landscape. It was bright enough to read the dial on our watches. The silence was broken by the baying of coyotes, letting us know that night creatures were around us. It wouldn't be the West without them. We call them night buglers!

Later we walked to the Rim again, peering into the deep abyss, and discovered that the moon had caught the ripples of the flowing Colorado, making it into a dancing stream. We were awed at the magnificence of it all, loathe to turn in for the night. We realized, as we made up our Jeep bed, that we were absolutely happy with this exciting adventure. Here we were in a place that the Indians called Toroweap and the breeze was wafting us to sleep with the tangy fragrance of its placename, *greasewood*..

Next morning we were at the Rim by dawn, just letting our sight penetrate down into the depths. We spent much of the day there, writing and reading, and looking.

It was down somewhere in this area at the bottom of this mighty slit that Major John Wesley Powell and his party, in 1869, had found evidence of volcanic action and enormous lava flows. As we sat there, in complete isolation and just a little bit lonely, we thought about those early explorers.

Powell, we feel, has scarcely been given the full credit he deserves for the enormity of his achievements. He was the first navigator of the Colorado. His daring exploits — conquering the wild rapids of an unknown mighty river — place him among the heroes of American exploration. If he did not actually give the Canyon its name he was the one who popularized it in his reports, until this became *Grand Canyon*.

He was founder and director of both the United States Geological Survey and the Bureau of American Ethnology. The value of his contributions to the study of the American Indians cannot be measured.

He established the system of geological and topographical maps that are still in use.

He became the most influential scientist in government in his time.

It all seemed so long ago, but time is a relative quality, especially in the Grand Canyon. Francis' geology professor at the University of Michigan, Professor William H. Hobbs, had once been an associate of Major Powell. Hobbs' book, which Francis studied, had many references to Powell and to the Canyon.[3] Our

110

Memorials to the Colorado River's first navigator are found in several places at Grand Canyon. This plaque is on the South Rim.

dear friend, the late Dr. Frederick Hodge, former director of the Los Angeles Southwest Museum, had often assisted Powell, and had given one of the eulogies at his memorial service on September 26, 1902 — the day Francis' brother (see chapter 1) was born.

(In 1984 we had a letter from Dr. Hodge's widow, Gene, in which she recounted an interesting episode at Grand Canyon. She wrote: "Fred and I spent ten days at the North Rim in 1941. Major Powell's daughter was there at the same time. A pipe burst in her cottage and flooded it. With a great sense of humor she said, 'Now I can imagine I am on the river with my father.'")

Corle's book was on the front seat of our Jeep and Helen opened it to the last page of the Toroweap chapter. "To stand at Toroweap Point is a requisite for anyone who wants to qualify for the degree of Grand Canyon graduate. It is the last and highest class that the school has to offer."

We felt that we at least partly deserved the degree of Grand Canyon graduates, although there were still so many things about it to learn and experience. Like most graduates, we knew there were years before we would finish our postgraduate work. Knowledge of and about the Canyon is a lifelong occupation. Anyone who has walked the trails, visited the viewpoints, studied the Canyon and its history, geology, and all the other ologies, will never be the same. It surely changes one into a better human being. It is possible to bow in gratitude to a *Canyon* for all the knowledge it has imparted.

Next morning, for over an hour, back in Mattie Kent's kitchen, we partook of a graduation breakfast.

XX

Grand Canyon Retreat
by Helen

1956

On an early April evening in 1956 we pulled our battered
Jeep into Cameron trading post, on the Little Colorado River. We
were headed for Grand Canyon Village, 60 miles west. We liked
Cameron in those days; a good place to spend the night.

Navajos and Hopis padded softly about their tasks. One of
them came from the tiny post office next to the trading post to
lower the American flag, which rippled in a gentle east wind.

After sunset, and just before dark, we walked out along the
high rock bluff back of the post, which gave a view down to the
tree-lined sandy shore of the Little Colorado. A dim path was
faintly visible, threading its way between giant brown boulders.
We scrambled down it, winding our way through a growth of
tamarisk trees, waving gently in the evening breeze and tossing
their soft pink-purple blossoms much as a horse flips its flowing
mane. Through rocks and brush we reached the river. Dozens of
times we had seen this Little Colorado with almost no water at
all. But this time! There had been flooding rains, and great melt-
offs of winter snows near its source. The river was wide and deep
— and swift. The waters were as chocolate brown as though a

devil's food cake had melted and started running. Molten, swift-flowing liquid mud. But as beautiful as a river of gold.

Night was sweeping in swiftly. The sky was an impressionist — almost a surrealist — painting of dark patterns in blocked, grotesque shapes of clouds. There was a single jagged opening, like the crudely shaped "light and air" windows of the ancient Indian ruins hereabout. Through this we could see the fingernail moon.

Next day, 15 miles west, just off the road to Grand Canyon, we stood at the "Viewpoint Turnout," gazing down into the gorge of dizzying depths, which the Little Colorado had carved through its multi-million year life.

How could one comparatively small section of America, we wondered, be so blessed as to have all the miracles of this canyon country which surrounded us? If this scene below were not overshadowed by its big sister, the Grand Canyon, such a short distance away — if this gash and gorge were in some prairie state in splendid isolation, it would be the focal point for half the continent. Now, it is just a hesitation along the way. Many tourists speed by without even stopping to discover its existence.

The great gash was so deep that we had to lean far out in some places — which added a touch of excitement to it all — in order to see the river twisting its way below. It was one of those "oh" and "ah" views.

This was, in fact, a natural, unstructured "Sight and Sound" display such as are now engineered throughout the world. The river, suddenly thrust into that narrow slit of rocks below, snarled angrily at its unexpected confinement, and sent roars of rage echoing upward.

There were other sounds — soft wheezing emanations from an array of lively swifts which were darting, skimming, swooping down and back in those mysterious spaces of the gorge, intent on pursuit of insects.

A fine looking Navajo woman, with her small son, came and stood beside us and we all watched the drama of wings and water together. She told us the Navajo name of the birds.

The little boy pointed downward. Out of apparently solid rock, a lovely mallow plant was tossing its orange blossomed head in the wind. Perhaps one of those birds had dropped a seed

which had found lodging place in some tiny crack or fissure.
Sight and sound. Wings and water. Delicate flower and a
small boy filled with wonder. Francis, almost unconsciously under the spell of the enchanted moment, began whispering, aloud, the words of one of
the Navajo songs that we knew.

> *In beauty I walk.*
> *Beauty before me,*
> *Beauty behind me,*
> *Beauty above and about me.*
> *It is finished in beauty.*
> *I walk in beauty.*

The Navajo woman smiled in confirmation.
We were headed for the South Rim's Bright Angel Lodge,
where we had been invited to show our just completed Navajo
film, at a "Camps Farthest Out" retreat, led by Dr. Glenn Clark.
Clark was not only Professor of Creative Religious Living, he
was athletic coach and also Professor of English at Macalester
College in Minnesota.
One early morning the two of us joined a creative writing
class which he was leading. Fifteen or twenty of us gathered in
the spacious room whose large windows looked directly out over
the Canyon.
"I teach writing by a different method than usual," Dr.
Clark explained, and told us that his classes at small Macalester
College had had more of its writing efforts published than any
other similar classes in the land. Clark himself had authored more
than thirty books.
In a corner of the room, by the window looking out toward
the Canyon, a woman began softly strumming the strings of a
harp.
"I want you to relax completely," Dr. Clark continued, as
he directed us in some simple quieting-down exercises. "Free
your body of every tension. Free your mind of every thought or
worry. Let the superconsciousness take over."
"Now," he continued after some moments of silence,

115

accentuated only by the strumming of the harp, "Now take your paper and pencil, go quietly outside. Don't think, consciously, of anything to write. Just put down on your paper what flows into you. Or through you. Come back in 25 minutes."

I had never written much, other than letters and college themes, in my life; had never even thought of writing a poem. I went out by the Canyon's Rim, looked out over the distance toward the Navajo reservation where we had spent so much of the last two years, and transferred onto paper the thoughts which floated in out of the stillness. I called it "Song of the Harp and the Loom," and Glenn Clark told us, after we had reassembled, to spend the rest of the hour in sharing, that each line which had come to me was filled with beauty, and was the finest expression of the creative writing hour.

These were the opening words of the three-page poem.

O, golden instrument of strings
Speak to us in rhythms bold and free
In songs of patterned harmony.

O, instrument of clear majestic song
You are the loom the Indians weave upon;
Your strings become the warp
Hung from poles of roughened bark.

Weave O Harpist of the early morn
As the Ancient One the rug,
Music of the High Plateau
And the chanting Navajo.

One of the Grand Canyon's important contributions to our lives — surely it was a highlight — was the inspiration which it generated in me, under Glenn Clark's direction, to attempt creative writing. Years later, we had a full-length book, consisting principally of poetry, published by Doubleday.[1] We have coauthored a number of books. That early morning hour, looking out over the Canyon's South Rim from Bright Angel Lodge, was the beginning, for me.

This Navajo weaver, a friend of the Lines, was an inspiration for Helen's first poem, written at Grand Canyon.

Another gift of that creative Grand Canyon experience was a rare friendship which has added sparkle to our lives for over a quarter century. Many friendships resulted from that experience, but this one was rooted in the land of the Canyon itself. From her home under a great cottonwood tree in the Hopi village of Oraibi, just east of Grand Canyon, had come a remarkable Hopi Indian woman, Polingaysi, or Elizabeth White, to use her anglicized name. She had been born in Old Oraibi, an Indian village dating back to 1100 A.D., the oldest continuously occupied place in North America. She had looked down from Old Oraibi's plateau to a spot which she loved and where, so she dreamed, she would one day build a beautiful home. That dream came true.

Polingaysi went to college, she became a teacher, medals and honor awards were bestowed on her. Her dream became concrete (or rather, adobe); she built her home at her dream spot and there entertained writers, painters, educators, sculptors, men and women of achievement who were creating dreams of their own.

When we first met Polingaysi at Grand Canyon she was a composer, pianist and vocalist, but not a potter. She started studying the art shortly after we met her; she became one of the Hopi Nation's most famous workers in clay. Her creations soared in value; they were sought after by collectors and museums. Other high honors came to her through the years and we were thrilled to be invited to contribute to a book published to celebrate her 90th birthday. Her own life story had been told in her own book, NO TURNING BACK.[2]

Polingaysi, in that creative writing class on Grand Canyon's Rim, symbolically portrayed a juniper tree which she observed growing from a Canyon crevice, valiantly struggling to exist. One brief statement in it characterizes her own life, which was nourished and brought to fruition in the frugal rocky soil of this land surrounding Grand Canyon:

"The most essential thing is to make sure that your roots are deep within the bosom of your mother earth and your arms continually lifted upward to heaven . . ."

A juniper tree, with roots breaking through the rocks, inspired a Hopi woman at a Grand Canyon writing session.

XXI

Down — and Out.
Rim to Rim
by Helen

1963

"Too bad we don't have a thermometer. It must be nearly freezing," I chattered through my teeth to Francis as we prepared to start down the North Kaibab Trail from Grand Canyon's North Rim. The day was June 4; the time about 4:30 a.m.

"How about this? It *is* freezing," came Francis' rejoinder a few minutes later. "Look, there's a scum of ice on that water."

Grey light had just begun creeping into the sky. Our sweaters and windbreakers had little effect in keeping out the chill. Francis, a native Michigander, didn't mind at all. But I was born and raised in central Arizona. I was *cold*.

Many hours — and 14 miles — later, down at Phantom Ranch close to the Colorado River, there *was* a thermometer. The temperature was 110° — in the shade of the cottonwoods that bordered Bright Angel Creek.

We had experienced just one more aspect and superlàtive of this incredible Canyon — a soaring in temperature of 80 degrees in a few hours, in traveling from Rim to River. I had long since learned that it is hard to avoid superlatives in Grand Canyon. It is hard, too, to avoid adventures when traveling with Francis. We were planning on a two-day hike, from Rim to Rim. Phone communications before leaving home a few days earlier had brought the bad news that Phantom Ranch, usual stop for overnighters down below, had no room left; reservations for that place should be made months in advance. We would have to camp out. But we were assured that we could eat there. That was good to learn. Francis was certain that I could make the long hike even if I had a few secret doubts.

I was really proud, as we signed the hikers' register at trail's head:

"Francis and Helen Line, Capistrano Beach, California. Hiking across to the South Rim, via the Kaibab Trail, June 4, 1963."

We were celebrating our 35th wedding anniversary, a month belatedly, because the North Rim trails were not open on May 1, our actual anniversary day.

Cold yet confident, we headed down — down through pines and aspens — and enormity. Fragrance of high mountain air filled us in great draughts, as a chill wind whistled a tune about our ears.

Gradually, some shafts of sunlight began seeping into our newfound world, spotlighting the surrounding cliffs. All was still and expectant. A cloudless sky stretched high above. It was a perfect day for adventure.

We took long gliding steps, trying out our legs on the unfamiliar trail, and were grateful for deep, soft dust which cushioned our feet. Sudden stops were hard to make but necessary as we came "head on" into vistas of tremendous depths — and heights — colored in all shades of reds and blues and whites. Every stop was a breathtaker.

We were dropping fast through millions of years, through Permian time, when seashells, ferns, and large animals inhabited this region. Evidences of bygone days were recorded in sandstone and rock.

The steepness of the grade pulled us downward like an invisible magnet, keeping us moving so fast that we didn't see the details at first. We were just conscious of the vastness and greatness of it all. But gradually we slowed down to admire the flowers which began to festoon our path. Wisteria-like vines with soft lavender colors, plants resembling night blooming datura, yellow daisies, and a few scarlet buglers. All of these added a softening touch to the rugged scene.

I had never before attempted this extensive a Canyon hike. Francis did everything to favor me. He carried the heavy pack, with all our extras of clothing, socks, first aid equipment, a gallon of water, rice, raisins, and the classified section of the Los Angeles Time.

"Why the Times? Why the classified section?" I wanted to know. "Do you think we might need to consult the 'Help Wanted' column?"

Francis laughed, then responded with a serious answer. "We've got to sleep down there tonight you know. Sleeping bags are heavy. Newspapers will help cut the chill."

We spoke of the possibility of being "dragouts," the term applied to those who have to send for a mule to bring them out if they become exhausted. In the freshness of the morning, this seemed remote.

Zigging and zagging, the trail dropped swiftly and we were soon within sound of "Roaring Springs," a beautiful swish of foaming water cascading down a steep canyon wall. Longingly we looked across the deep chasm and wished for a drink of the precious liquid, but decided against the trip down for it would have added more distance to our hike. Instead, we took the righthand fork of the trail, marked "Power House, one mile." Beside us now were pipes, part of the engineering system by which drinking water is carried up to the Rim.

Bidding good-bye to the gnarled old juniper trees as we descended deeper into the Canyon, we exchanged them for a stand of gorgeously blooming Apache plume — feathery and soft to the touch. A huge cactus plant spread protective hands at the gateway to the power house. Then — a welcome but almost ridiculous sight. There before us was a modern drinking fountain.

Ridiculous or not, we almost ran to reach it and were soon relishing drinks of real Grand Canyon spring water. My knees were trembling as we luxuriated in the refreshing pause; — holding back on the downward plunge is sometimes harder than climbing.

We sat briefly, looking up, quenching our thirst and absorbing the beauty of our surroundings. The sheer red cliffs of massive formations towered above us, the rushing sound of Bright Angel Creek filled our ears. It was to be our "music of the trail" for most of the remaining day.

Slowly we drifted down an easier incline, which leveled out gradually as we entered the Sonoran Zone. Our vistas were up now. The majesty of peaks, temples, thrones, and domes were visible to us. We skirted the base of a great rock mass, passed other fine formations which were hard to identify. It was absolutely tremendous to be a wayfarer on this almost holy ground. We had the feeling that God's creation is still going on, and will be into eternity.

Desert vegetation was plentiful in this area. Yucca in bloom, blossoming cactus, sage, and agave. Cottonwood trees kept their feet in cool, galloping Bright Angel Creek and made a pattern of shimmering green the entire length of the lower canyon. We crossed and recrossed the creek on small plank suspension bridges, or in shallow places jumped from boulder to boulder.

Twice we came upon surveyors close to Cottonwood Camp, the home for the workers of the trail. A public camp is also available here. The men were laying out a new pipeline from Roaring Springs.

We were "down in" — looking up, seeing the Grand Canyon from new angles. Experiencing it, feeling it, hearing it, contemplating its history and struggle to be born. We sat silently and let the drama of it all flow around us. Words were extraneous. We would be different for having experienced this adventure. Hiking is surely the way to do it. One needs the textures of the trail, the deep soft dust, the fine-ground buoyant stone path, the gravel, the hard rocks, the mile on mile of downhill pull, the quietness, the lilting joy of Bright Angel's cascading waterfalls. These can best be seen and felt on foot, slowly, with time to digest their message.

We had to crawl over huge boulders for quite a distance off the trail to find "Ribbon Falls."

I was reluctant to attempt the extra hiking but, in this

instance, Francis was adamant.

"When my brother and I first came to Grand Canyon, and heard the government lecture," he explained, "the ranger rolled a phrase off his tongue which we could never forget. He said one of the great sights of the Canyon was 'Ribbon Falls on Angel Creek.'"

Francis explained that the ranger had accented the first syllable of Ribbon and of Angel, making it almost like a phrase of music, which he and his brother had repeated for days. He was insistent that we set eyes on the inspiration for that ranger's lilting phrase.

I was glad that Francis had been adamant. That extra few minutes of boulder hopping carried us into a musical fairyland. A gossamer sheet of water, sprayed out by the wind, has dropped through the centuries down onto a veritable king's throne, now moss covered, at its base. "A thing of beauty is a joy forever," came to mind as we viewed it. This has been here for an eternity for all to see who pass this way. Perhaps it's more beautiful because not too many see it. It is completely unspoiled. Quiet shadows of boulders and trees cooled us as we rested. Tiny tree frogs were sunning themselves on rocks below the falls. One of them was emitting a subtle sound." I think I know what he's saying," suggested Francis."He's repeating, 'Rib'bon Falls on An'gel Creek,'"

As we regained the main trail, and continued downward, occasional lizards, as large as Mexican iguanas, darted across our path. Animal tracks were numerous — deer, ringtails, foxes, and rabbit — but the lizards were the only ones brave enough to enjoy our company.

Going on, a sign told us we were looking at some of the older rocks on this earth. One should say "in this earth," for these rocks were formed far below the surface. They were of the Archean period, the era of geological time in which this granite gorge, which we were now entering, was formed, some two billion years ago. Imagine this little Bright Angel Creek cutting its way through these gigantic formations to expose these ancient rocks, originally composed of layers on layers laid down both on land and in the sea. They are no longer recognizable in their original forms, because of the tremendous pressures and heat to

The gentle waters of Ribbon Falls drop out of a high crevasse onto moss-covered rocks below, as Helen watches.

126

When viewed at close range, "Ribbon Falls on Angel Creek" appears to be descending onto a king's throne.

127

which they have been subjected for a couple of billion years. These concepts became the ingredients of mind-boggling meditation as we quietly drifted on through this Methuselahn area. Going first on one side of the creek and then the other, with the walls rising higher and higher and the space between them growing narrower and narrower, we felt squeezed in. The last five miles, even though mostly level, were the hardest of the day, for the heat was becoming intense. And we were *tired*. Tired not alone physically, but mentally as well. Trying to come to grips with a two billion-year-old environment into which you are suddenly thrust requires an enormous feat of mental gymnastics. As bend after bend in the canyon walls failed to reveal Phantom Ranch, we finally lay down beside the creek in a small stretch of sand and rocks, and let our bodies — and our minds — go limp.

It was only after reaching Phantom Ranch that we discovered that the afternoon temperature was 110°. It was probably good that we hadn't known how hot it actually was. Later still, we learned that heat of this kind, recorded on a thermometer at eye level in Grand Canyon, can translate into a temperature of nearly 200° at ground level, where rocks reflect the rays of the sun. (See Chapter 37) Had we known that fact, we probably would not have lain down as we rested.

A human voice brought us suddenly back to twentieth century reality. The first hiker we had encountered all day — he was on his way up to the North Rim — stopped to say "hello."

Our surprise guest was a young Polish mathematician, in America on a one year teaching assignment at Notre Dame. Figuratively we tipped our hats to him as we learned that he was hiking across the Canyon just to save bus fare to the North Rim and other points of interest.

By midafternoon — approximately 3 p.m. — as the shadows in this deep Canyon were already beginning to lengthen, a grove of cool cottonwoods told us that our day's hike of 14 miles was nearly completed. Francis even thought that he recognized the spot where, 40 years ago, he and his brother had been entertained with the sounds of what they thought was a wildcat.

There were no such sounds this time. But soon we heard voices — and the sounds of mules. Then we came to small

Francis, with heavy pack, follows Bright Angel Creek between massive walls of rock which are two billion years old.

cabins, and a dining lodge.

This was Phantom Ranch.

I lay down to rest while Francis went to find out when the dinner hour would be. Five minutes later he came back.

"Damn," was, at first, his only word.

"What's wrong?"

"They're too crowded. They won't feed us."

"But — they told us . . . . "

"No — the people that we phoned up on the Rim told us. Those people forgot to notify Phantom Ranch. They've got too many people here already. An extra mule train came in. I guess they're low on supplies."

Perhaps we might have pleaded our case in another try. But Francis was a bit disgusted.

"Look, we've got some rice. Why don't we cook it? The weather's going to be even hotter tomorrow. Why don't we eat some rice, take a good rest, then try hiking on out tonight?"

"You mean by dark? Hike the whole Canyon in one day? You've got to be kidding."

I was the one who finally said, "Yes, let's try it. We'll have something to talk about when we get home."

"*If* we get home," I added, a bit grimly.

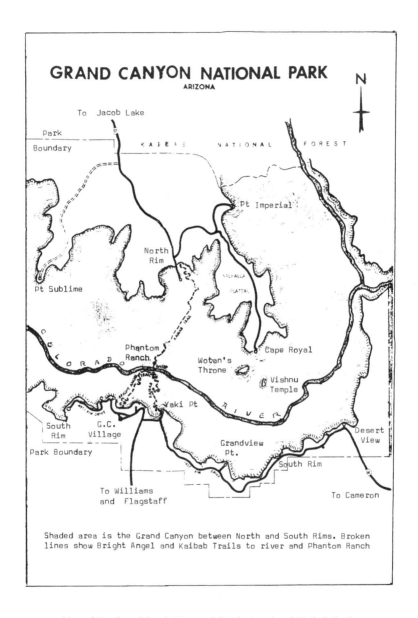

Map of North and South Rims and Bright Angel and Kaibab Trails.

XXII

Adventure by Night
by Helen

We sat silently for awhile, waiting to cool off, physically, and mentally. No food for us at the Inn. Only a cup of rice and some raisins in our pack. We said, "Let's take a shower and really cool off." It was an antidote for our disappointment. The cool water soothed our tiredness. We felt refreshed in body, mind, and spirit, and ready for our next move.

Francis started unpacking while I gathered a few dry sticks along Bright Angel Creek for a small fire.[1] Our rice and raisins, cooked in an empty coffee can, tasted like gourmet food. And what a restaurant we had. A special seat beside Bright Angel Creek, under the cottonwoods at Phantom Ranch, with great cliffs rising around us, purpling in the setting sun.

An excitement took hold of us around the glowing coals. We were absolutely on our own now — no meals to wait for at Phantom Ranch. We had made it down on our own; cooked the little food we had. We felt as free as the wind which was rising.

We decided then and there to rest a little longer, then in the cool of the evening to start up the Kaibab Trail to the South Rim. We would hike it by the light of the moon. How fortunate we were to have decided on this trip to the Canyon during its full phase. We paid attention to the warning — one gallon of water for each person climbing up the Kaibab Trail. We filled all our canteens and plastic water bottles, putting them in the pack. We put on our boy scout belts and tried out the canteens on them. They felt extremely heavy, but it did not discourage us.

Our muscles were stiff from the three hour rest, so we lazed along to the bridge, and began to feel in good hiking form. The long shadows of evening enveloped us. The sun's last gold lighted the graceful narrow suspension bridge high above the river. Slowly we crossed over and commenced the arduous climb of a trail that rose straight up, up into the gathering night. The last rays of sun touched the surrounding temples and peaks, as we picked up speed and found according to the mile post that we were ticking off a mile an hour. We needed this encouragement.

Each zigzag was a stop for breath and a drink, and a chance for reflection. We took this time also to let Francis down to a seat on a rock, with his heavy pack and canteens, so he could really rest. Then adjusting the pack and a heavy pull to get him up again was a major task. We had just finished the hardest 14 mile hike of my life, yet here we were tackling one of the steepest trails in the Canyon, up the zigging and zagging Kaibab Trail. Two people going into the vastness of the night following a moonbeamed trail. At points we were dazzled by its splendor. On the dark side of the mountain we used a flashlight. Deep chasms dropped sheer beside us. A sharp cold wind plagued us. We began putting on our windbreakers, then an extra sweater, which we had not expected to don this early.

This night experience thrilled us. There was a feeling of loneliness, yet a closeness to God. Each zigzag was one more rise on our way to the top. My inner thoughts were zigging and zagging also. I was joyful at being able to be on this great night adventure, yet at times I'd feel so tired and cold I would ask Francis to stop so we could lie down and rest. We'd try to find a rock that would shield us from the wind.

Night soundlessness wrapped itself around us. Not even a cricket chirping. We felt at times we were the only living things on the Kaibab Trail.

Then suddenly, animal shapes in the night. Once Francis saw a great mountain cat slip silently into the blackness, not telling me until a long time afterwards. My sudden fear on a treacherous turn, with the wind whipping in from all sides. We stopped, took off the packs, got out the classified ad section of the Los Angeles Times, God bless it, and put sheets of it under our jackets, and we felt much warmer. Best use I've ever made of the want-ads.

Flashlights piercing the blue-blackness of the night. Amazing brilliance of the moon, eclipsing the stars. Great shadows looming ahead. Drinking water on the long pulls and breathing hard but feeling tremendously alive and happy to be there . . . on the trail! Always feeling that we were going to top out onto a level area. If the trail *did* level out, in the darkness we failed to observe it. Nothing can approximate the wonder of that moonlight experience. It was truly a night of enchantment, hard but exciting and surely different from the humdrum of daily life.

There was no way to gauge how far we'd hiked; we only knew the moon was gliding across the heavens, each hour going down a little more. My flashlight gave out and suddenly I was caught in a precarious spot. It seemed that the trail was on a peninsula and dropping off on both sides. I got down on my hands and knees and fearfully crawled to where there seemed to be more safety.

We were icy cold when we made it up the steep grade to Cedar Ridge. We knew then how far it was to the top — only one-and-a-half miles farther to go. We found a sheltered spot under a shaggy juniper and curled up, with our raincoats for better protection, and actually slept for over an hour. It was so good to be rid of the canteens and to lie quiet. Blessed rest!

When we awoke we were ravishingly hungry. We got out the remainder of the cooked rice which we had saved in case we felt the need of food, and ate it. Rice does satisfy even when cold. We felt refreshed.

It was completely dark for a short while after the moon set. But not for long. The sun's power began to be felt long before we actually saw it. A gradual turning to gold, then pink, and a new dawn was upon us. We gazed all around locating temples and points of interest and even looking back at the North Rim where we'd been just 24 hours ago. It was a new world, shining in all its

The sunrise, after their Rim to Rim crossing of Grand Canyon in one day and night, seemed to Francis and Helen the most beautiful they had ever experienced.

morning glory.

We started up the steep ascent as dawn crept in and soon a mule train of supplies was upon us, with orders first to take to the outside. It was a long sharp drop-off and we clung precariously there while three mules passed. Then a stubborn one balked and the wrangler instructed us to take the inside, which we gratefully did. We watched, fascinated as the mules took the sharp V's on the steep downgrade, with the trail literally carved out of the face of the rock walls. A breathtaking sight. That was the trail we had come up in the dark! J. B. Priestley, the English author, who loved the Grand Canyon, was right: "Arizona is geology by day and astronomy by night." We had experienced it all in just 24 hours. We made the last zigzags and topped out at 5:30 a.m. Twenty-two miles in all, from dawn to dawn.[2]

Francis smiled at me and patted my arm as he said, "Helen, you were no drag-out! And aren't you glad Phantom Ranch wouldn't feed us?" Yes, I was glad, for this wasn't just a hike, it was a once-in-a-lifetime adventure. It was finding a new dimension in time and space. It was truly seeing, in a way we'd never experienced it before, THE GRAND CANYON OF ARIZONA.

XXIII

Cow Pasture Landing
by Helen

"So near and yet so far." We had hiked the Canyon, Rim to Rim, 22 miles,[1] in one day. But the trip back to our car, by road, would be 215 miles. Now we realized the North Rim ranger's predicament on election days. He could see his voting booth, at El Tovar on the South Rim, but to drive there and cast his ballot was a 430-mile round trip. Luckily for us, an informal plane service was available.

The airstrip was far south of Grand Canyon Village, reached by a taxi ride longer than the distance over to the North Rim itself. The plane was so tiny that the pilot and Francis had no trouble pushing it out of the hangar and onto the airstrip. We had to crowd to get ourselves and our gear all in; the pilot exchanged a good-bye wave with the mechanic back at the hangar, and we circled out over the Canyon.

Grand Canyon by air. We had viewed it from half a hundred different vantage points along the Rim, providing us with the surface view. We had penetrated its interior by hiking down and in, which was like seeing an X ray slide revealing the Canyon's innards. Now came this scanning overall survey from above. I

139

leaned forward to take a picture. Whipping wind and throbbing motor jarred the camera. I tried to steady myself.

"Say, Sam, did you check the motor of this thing last night?"

It was the pilot's voice, speaking over the radio — obviously with the mechanic back at the hangar. For the first time, as we caught what he was saying, we realized that the plane's motor was sputtering, even missing some strokes. We had been so completely lost in the Canyon's depths down below that we had not thought about being aloft in the frail flying machine — with an uncertain motor.

"Did you go over it?" Our pilot repeated his question. Where we had been all eyes, we were now all ears. From our pilot's expression, we gathered that Sam had failed to go over the motor.

I never finished taking the picture. Lucky we had gotten as uninterrupted a view down below as we had enjoyed *before* the pilot started checking with Sam. After that, our main interest in what lay down there was to see how quickly the North Rim would replace that rock-ribbed gorge as our "safety net" in case of a forced landing.

The plane had made slow time to begin with; we had been overjoyed at that, for it afforded more opportunity to absorb the wonders below from our flying carpet in the sky. Now, with motor sputtering, the tiny plane didn't even seem to be moving — except to be slowly sinking. North Rim at last, but only pine trees below. Now we were barely skimming their tops. Then a cow pasture, or I guess it was a natural Kaibab Forest meadow. It looked like a cow pasture, and felt like one, as we jolted to a scary landing and came to a stop.

"Little motor trouble," explained the pilot, with no more concern than a housewife would have had if the bobbin of her sewing machine acted up. "I don't know why Sam slipped up on it the way he did."

In 15 minutes the park ranger, summoned by radio, was pulling beside us in his truck and in another 15 minutes he had kindly driven us out to where we had left our car near the head of Kaibab Trail.

Our complete physical weariness from crossing the Grand

140

Canyon on foot in one day, and without sleep now for 32 hours, had been erased temporarily by the pinging of the airplane motor and the pilot's chilling radio conversation with Sam. That episode added some emotional tension to muscle strain and as we drove silently north toward Kanab our exhaustion was nearly total. With real effort we avoided checking in at the first motel we came to in Kanab, but wisely hunted around for nearly half an hour until we located a small place two or three blocks off the main highway, where quietness would assure us not only a good night's sleep but also a preliminary nap for the remainder of this day. It was now about 3 p.m.

A tub shower — and we needed it. A sigh of joyous exhaustion. Then to bed and oblivion.

And then, a *wail*. A scream. Pounding on doors. More wailing. Beyond the partition of our room — in the next quarters apparently — some family crisis or subhuman melodrama, we couldn't tell what, was spiraling into an awful climax. We probably heard the first parts of it in our sleep — — some ghastly nightmare. Now we were both very wide awake, trying to remember where we were — and why.

Some child in the next apartment, we finally concluded, had locked himself in the bathroom. By the sound of his crying, and his inability to follow any of the frantically yelled directions from his parents, obviously he was too young to know what was being said. Or too scared to understand. We took it for granted that it was a "he." No girl baby could have produced such wild screams.

By examining our own bathroom door we soon realized what had doubtless happened. The inner knob lock had been turned, the child had shut the door, and he did not understand how to unlock it from the inside. That was the only place from which it *could* be unlocked. The door had no place for a key.

The adults next door hadn't figured that out yet.

"Go get the manager," someone screamed. "Get a key."

The manager had gone to town. The screaming continued.

First it just continued. Then it got worse. Soon the child was hysterical and Francis and I realized that this was not just a weird incident; it might soon be deadly serious.

"There's an outside window; let's break it," came a voice

141

which must have been the mother's.

"But the falling glass. It'd hit Brent. It could kill him."

That, logically and obviously, was the father.

The manager showed up — a woman. With ladder and screwdriver, all of them working together removed the outside window, and a little sister of the distressed family was lowered into the bathroom and to the rescue.

Francis and I, weary, groggy, incredulous, but completely in the grip of insomnia, went out to supper. It was probably 10 o'clock that night before we went to bed, with as big a list of subject matter for nightmares as we had ever had in one day and night. But we never even dreamt. We slept until a cleaning woman rattled our door at 11 o'clock next morning. That, we discovered, was checking out time.

The balance of this book
has been written by
Francis and Helen together

142

XXIV

Johnnie Discovers the Canyon

by Francis and Helen

1965, and later.

First impressions are vital.

A psychiatrist, Leonard Zunin, M. D., has written a book titled CONTACT: THE FIRST FOUR MINUTES. The title explains itself. When persons meet for the first time, says the doctor, it takes only a few minutes — usually about four — for them to decide whether or not they are interested in one another.

What applies to persons can also be true for relationships with *things* — cars, cities, razors, or chewing gum. If, on your first visit to a restaurant, you are served a bowl of soup with a fly in it, you may loathe the place forever. If the soup is flavorful, delicious, you are apt to return.

With this concept of the importance of first impressions in mind, when we took our young grandchildren on their initial visit to Grand Canyon we did not plan it like a visit to Disneyland — packed parking lots, popcorn, free balloons, and roar of bands and traffic. We drove them through the pines approaching South Rim, detoured far off to a special solitary viewpoint we knew of,

The authors' grandchildren, Jeff and Jan, absorb the Grand Canyon view.

walked through the silent forests together and stepped out to the Rim.

Our six-year-old grandson looked out, looked back and up at us and uttered one word: "Wow!" That may possibly stand as the shortest yet most emotion-packed description of the Canyon which has ever been given.

This quiet approach is in some degree the manner in which Francis and his brother had had their first impressions of the Canyon, in the simple days of the early 1920s.

In contrast, on one of our recent visits, we followed an Indiana couple and their young children as they came to Grand Canyon for the first time, approaching it from Cameron and stopping at Desert View for their initial exploration. This is the point at which a great many of the visitors obtain their first Canyon vista.

Just to get a parking space, even before the exploration began, was a fender-bending experience. The toilets came next — waiting in line, flush and swirl, drying the hands to the whir of an electric motor and a jet of hot air.

Then the grocery store, gift and souvenir shop, and a cafe and quick snack place.

"Double-dips, look daddy, they've got double-dips."

"Not now," answered daddy. "Come look at this statue." He was examining two wooden, gaudily painted statues, out in front of the store, lining the sidewalk leading toward the Rim. One statue was of a mountain man, the other of a western gambler.

But the child's teasing persisted and both he and his sister soon had chocolate ripple double-dips.

"You can't take those into the gift shop," their mother warned. "Don't you see the sign? You stay outside. I want to buy a little present for Alice."

The asphalt sidewalk from parking lot to Rim led past a gauntlet of Pepsi and Coke machines, an ice dispenser, snack bar, and a neatly-constructed trash receptacle where, hopefully, some of the remainders of the snacks could find a resting place.

The Rim at last? No, not quite. At Desert View, this first stopping place for all those millions who approach from the east, by way of Cameron, the Canyon is most often viewed, not from

145

the actual Rim itself, but from the great view windows or the observation roof of the Watchtower, which dominates the landscape. This tower — of Hopi Indian design — is a work of art, with educational displays as one climbs to the top. We salute it. But anyone entering the tower for his initial view of Grand Canyon first has to salute something else. Many something elses. The whole ground floor — the room which the hopeful viewer must enter — is a colossal souvenir shop. The Indiana mother needn't have been in such haste to purchase her present for Alice; she would have a far greater assortment to choose from, here.

"Look, we can use our Mastercharge," called out her husband, reading a sign on the window beside the entrance door.

Just inside, to the left, the visitors from Indiana were greeted with the music of cash register bells, ringing up sales from the drink and snackfood displays flanking the way around the tower's leftside interior - dispensers of churning red punch and swirling yellow lemonade, two stands of chewing gum, displays of candy bars, Crackerjacks, lemondrops, and boxes of cheese nips, cheese tidbits, and Barnum's animal crackers.

That was the cash register for the snacks. The dominant bell-music came from the register mounted in the center of the great circular room which formed this view tower's ground floor. A seven-sided septagon of glass display cases was the centerpiece — seven cases of flashing jewelry, knickknacks, and trinkets.

Beyond this great central display, on the perimeters, were the view windows. But not quite yet time for the view.

Each great window had, in front of it, counters and stools of goods for sale. The choicest view windows (where many see the Canyon for the first time) were flanked and fronted with a five-shelf display of hand carved onyx from old Mexico (including dozens of identical pieces), — oxyx clocks, pots, figuerines, dolls. Squeezed amongst these were replicas of Navajo weaving and baskets, all price marked for sale. On ledges directly in front of each of the view windows, commanding part of your view as you looked, were boxes of pieces and bits of polished rocks (each piece with a large square price tag), piles of Gallup throw rugs, hunks of small flat rocks with paintings on each, and three-tiered displays of books and tiny souvenir drums. Nearly everything was in dozen or half-gross quantities.

146

"Look, mama, look at all these dolls," called out the little girl from Indiana, above the clatter of the register bells. "Golly, I didn't know the Grand Canyon would be like this."

The girl was in ecstacies over the dolls — cloth dolls, plaster of Paris dolls, wax dolls. She hadn't seen the Canyon yet.

"Oh, look," called her brother, "there it is."

Little Johnnie from Indiana had discovered Grand Canyon. John Wesley Powell had had to run treacherous rapids to have his first view of the Canyon. The early Spaniards had had to undergo hardships of mountains and deserts. Johnnie from Indiana had had to run a gauntlet almost as severe, and only came upon the view of the Canyon by chance — through a welter of Barnum's animal crackers, onyx clocks, and Gallup throw rugs.

Initial views are important. By the time Johnnie's first casual, almost accidental — most certainly incidental — view of the Canyon was mixed with the lather of Coke machines, swirling red punch, gewgaws and fribbles and baubles — his concept of the Canyon was in all likelihood more circuslike than Grand.

"What's the Grand Canyon like?" his friends and school-mates back home will ask him next autumn. If he had ever heard of that line from Gilbert and Sullivan he could, with some truth, use it in a reply:

"The time has come, the walrus said, to speak of many things, of chewing gum and sealing wax, of cabbages and kings."

Chewing gum and sealing wax may well have been his lasting impression.

Francis and Helen's grandchildren see the Watchtower at Grand Canyon's Desert View.

From an observation window high up in the tower, Jan and Jeff look down at the Colorado River.

XXV

Red Rock Trail to Supai

1975, and later.

"One of the most beautiful waterfalls in all America." That was Francis' excited assessment of Havasu Falls, hidden from the world a couple of miles below the Havasupai Indian village in the remote lower reaches of Grand Canyon. He was speaking not alone of the cascading waters — tumbling down like streams of spilled turquoise beads — but of the rock-enclosed turquoise pools which those waters formed below, and of the stalactite-stalagmite travertine rocks over which those waters glided. Considering the superlative waterfalls which America has to display, at Niagara, in Yosemite and Yellowstone, along the Columbia River Highway, in Hawaii, and elsewhere, we felt that Francis' statement might be unduly colored by the excitement of the moment. Then we ran across a statement in Felton O. Gamble's book, EXPLORE GRAND CANYON: "Havasu Falls is one of the most beautiful sights of the entire world."[1]

Perhaps Francis, and also Felton Gamble, were both overstating the case for Havasu Falls. One fact is certain; this rock-rimmed turquoise gem is unique; no other waterfall has its special character.

Havasu and its sister waterfalls below the Indian settlement have drawn us four different times down to this Shangri-la of lower Grand Canyon. It is one of the Canyon's treasures which we did not discover until 1975, although we had first made plans to visit Supai 30 years before, to produce a color motion picture of the Indian life there, and its idyllic surroundings. H. C. Bryant, superintendent of Grand Canyon National Park, was co-operating with us on our project. He issued a park permit for filming professionally at Supai, indicating that we should contact the Agent there. But, he wrote us, "The Indians are amenable to photographer's wishes and gratuities are usually in the form of hard candy."

The Agent saw it otherwise. Erroneously gaining the impression that we were a large Hollywood company, he set a fee — to be paid to the Indians — which was beyond our means at that time. We gave up our filming plans. When finally we *did* visit Supai, accompanied by our two young granddaughters, and without the strain of carrying heavy camera equipment, or the tension of film production — when we *did* make our trip to Supai, we had no cares in the world except to absorb its beauty and its wonders, and become close friends — non-professionally — with the Indians.

Our 1975 autumn hike to the Indian village and the waterfalls began at Hualapi Hilltop, 68 miles — over mainly rugged dirt roads — from Peach Springs, Arizona. Desiring to start the downward trek at sunrise, we drove to Hilltop mainly by dark. Tortuous rocks and ruts made driving hard but we were rewarded — if that is the proper term — with a display of animal nightlife such as we had seldom seen before. Probably half a thousand jackrabbits, during the 68 mile drive, criss-crossed the road in front of our car. Perhaps a hundred of them, at one time or another, raced in front of us, attempting to escape our headlights. Their speed was electric. Streaking, long-eared bundles of fur seemed to fill our world.

When the grassy terrain merged into areas of junipers, then ponderosa pines, the rabbit rampage subsided. Then we merged into grasslands again, and more rabbits. They deserted us toward dawn; we dropped down into a circuitous gorge, and a slight climb brought us to Hualapi Hilltop, where 30 or more cars were parked. Munching a stand-up picnic breakfast, we looked down at as much of the trail as was visible. It was steep. A cruel, cold wind whipped across the Hilltop, swirling dirt and dust onto our food. We bundled up in extra sweaters, wondered a bit if the airy onslaught might blow us off the trail, and started down. At once, a sheer perpendicular white cliff began shielding us from the wind. The descent was steep; soon all gustiness of the air was gone. We entered a world of quiet; quietness of air movement, quietness of sounds. Extraneous noises were gone. The 30 parked cars were no longer visible. We four were the only signs of civilized life in this canyon world we were entering.

There *were* sounds, occasionally; our hiking boots clicking against native rocks, for this trail was almost a cobblestone affair — huge boulders, almost like flattened washtubs, embedded in it. But they afforded good boot holds on the steep descent.

Then — other sounds. A faint staccato of hooves behind us. The tattoo grew louder; looking back, we saw seven Indian ponies trotting toward us. They were unattended by any humans. Frightened at our presence, they veered from the trail, plunged down a ravine, made it up the far side, then fanned out onto a desert ridge of low growth, and disappeared. Where they had come from, where they went, we did not know. Our first mystery of this mysterious land.

Switchbacks in the trail zigzagged below us, so steep in places that care was required in going down. But up those switchbacks came a figure, running. Soon we could see that it was an Indian — a handsome young man negotiating the steep ascent with almost the speed of one of the jackrabbits we had chased. Our expressions of amazement brought a smile to his face, and our questioning greeting brought a response, as he hesitated briefly: "I go to Hilltop. Catch a ride into Peach Springs." Then he was gone — like a jackrabbit.

Our steep downward descent continued for a mile-and-a-half. Supai village is eight miles from Hilltop, with the last of the waterfalls three miles farther, and we wondered what the climb out might be, if it continued as steep as this. Then everything changed — abruptly.

A battered sign, "Supai," with an arrow pointing to the right, indicated that we should make a sharp right angle turn, to

153

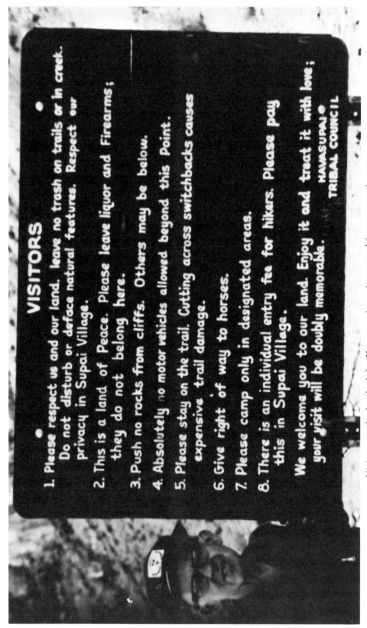

VISITORS

1. Please respect us and our land. Leave no trash on trails or in creek. Do not disturb or deface natural features. Respect our privacy in Supai Village.

2. This is a land of Peace. Please leave liquor and Firearms; they do not belong here.

3. Push no rocks from cliffs. Others may be below.

4. Absolutely no motor vehicles allowed beyond this Point.

5. Please stay on the trail. Cutting across switchbacks causes expensive trail damage.

6. Give right of way to horses.

7. Please camp only in designated areas.

8. There is an individual entry fee for hikers. Please pay this in Supai Village.

We welcome you to our land. Enjoy it and treat it with love; your visit will be doubly memorable.

HAVASUPAI
TRIBAL COUNCIL

Visitors to the land of the Havasupai are instructed in proper etiquette.

the north. A lone girl hiker, we later learned, had missed that sign and had wandered off in the other direction. She was found, weeks later, still alive.

Following the trail in its new course, we entered a red rock-rimmed canyon. The descent became gradual. The texture and nature of the material over which we were walking was revealed by another sign: "Warning: Trail Subject to Flash Floods." We were traversing, between these narrow red walls, what became, at times, a virtual riverbed. Where the canyon was wide enough, we had our choice of walking through loose sand, or over gravel, or even of picking our way around and over boulders, all products of flash flooding.

We stumbled often, over those boulders, for our eyes — far too frequently — were not on where our next step would be (as should have been the case) but on the majesties that were beginning to unfold, all about us. The rock canyon writhed like a serpent, so that we could seldom see more than a few hundred feet ahead. The views, rather, were *up*. Those red rock walls broke into fantastic shapes.

For our youngest granddaughter — eleven-year-old Krista — this was like Alice's adventures in Wonderland.

"Look, that big rock is a red frog; he's going to leap down on us."

"See those three rocks, as tall as chimneys. They look like ogres."

"That rock looks like a puppy."

Back beyond the red cliffs now began rising towering escarpments that were white. The sky — the narrow slit which we could see far above — was deep blue. Nature was displaying the national colors. As the canyon wound and undulated in its descent, it was as though those national colors were gently waving in the breeze.

Now the views were not alone up, but often to either side. To our right was a great burnt-red rock overhang. It would have made an excellent shelter from a thunderstorm, but no protection at all from the flash flood which such a thunderstorm might bring.

Soon, on our left, was a rock overhang which could shelter a regiment and which made us seem like dwarfs as we explored it.

155

It was as though we were within the broken half of a huge red urn.

Sounds, both ahead and behind us. From our shelter of rock, as though we had a grandstand seat, we watched two pack trains pass — one coming down with mail and supplies, the other a single Indian woman, with two extra horses, followed by two dogs. Later, an Indian man, coming down with a string of horses (but not the seven ponies we had seen) called out to us encouragingly, "You almost there, just four more miles."

One of his animals had been injured on a rock. For a mile or so we followed a trail of scattered blood drops.

The canyon narrowed to a slit corkscrewing its way so crazily that in places we could see only 50 feet ahead. At these narrow spots, the pungent odor of manure on the trail hung heavy in the air. At one narrow place a giant boulder had fallen; only a nine-foot passageway remained open. And at another, wider spot, so many room-sized rocks had tumbled from the cliffs above that the canyon was completely blocked. Passageway had been made by cutting a trail into the side of the canyon wall itself, above the height of the fallen boulders. Soon we came to an overhang of rocks which could almost have sheltered a small army.

With the imaginative aid of our granddaughters, we determined how this grotesque canyon might have been formed. Some legendary Pauline Bunyan, up on the Hualapi Hilltop, must have been brewing an enormous cauldron of chocolate fudge, when the pan ran over. The molten contents, spewing for six miles down the wash, all hardened into these giant red walls of every size and shape. These boulders must have been the nuts in the fudge.

Several groups of hikers passed us, coming up — the owners of those cars parked at Hilltop.

Suddenly there was water in the wash where we walked. Our descent became precipitous, dropping in giant steps, beside which were much larger giant rock and boulder steps over which the water coursed downward. In a flash flood, this would be a roaring waterfall. Cables were strung to aid passage up or down. This was the "ladder." Some animal — a squirrel perhaps? — far above, loosened a small rock and it crashed 30 feet ahead of us.

Our canyon widened. Its narrowness had closed us in so completely that here, for the first time, we saw the sun. A branch canyon came in from the right. Through cottonwoods ahead we saw and heard a stream — an undulating, bubbling ribbon of turquoise. This was Havasu Creek. We had reached the magic waters of Havasupai.

XXVI

The Legend of Havasu Canyon

Where the waters of Havasu Creek originate is not known for certain. But, even before continuing the mile-and-a-half downstream to Supai Village, we took steps to solve for ourselves, at least partially, the mystery of its origins. Heading upstream, we soon came to a beautiful pool, under the shade of a cottonwood tree. We followed on back, but there was only brackish water, standing in stagnant puddles. Beyond that, a completely dry wash. That glorious tree-shaded pool — fed, some speculate, by an underground flow from as far away as the San Francisco Peaks — that is the origin of the stream which provides life for the Indian village, and creates the waterfalls of Havasu Canyon.

A battered sign terminated this exploratory side trip: "Topocoba Hilltop, 14 miles. Trail not recommended."[1] This used to be the principal gateway to and from Supai but is now seldom used. An inexperienced hiker recently became lost in this area and was within a day or so of perishing when he was located. Turning back, we began following the stream toward the village.

Two Indian boys were shooting at a squirrel with a

slingshot. "You hit him?" Francis asked. "No," came the honest reply, accompanied by a broad smile.

Bird song began filling the air. The waters of the stream were likewise singing. Several times we crossed and recrossed on bridges formed of single logs. Each crossing required a balancing act. Some butterflies lazed their way back and forth without benefit of bridges.

The distant sound of barking dogs. As we passed between two boulders, the village began spreading before us, a green meadow sprinkled with fruit trees, small houses dotting the fields, and the two legendary towering rocks of Supai — of which we had read — rising over the left side of the canyon which enclosed this quiet splendor.

These rocks, so a legend goes, were once an Indian man and his spouse who, caught climbing out of the valley in search of some new paradise, were turned to stone by the gods. It was a warning, to others who might get the wanderlust, that no paradise as fine as this could be found beyond these canyon walls.

As we continued on and began absorbing the scene around us, that legend seemed less implausible than we had thought. Great cottonwoods lined the trail, which widened slightly to become the village's main street. This was October. Each cottonwood leaf was like a golden flame; each great tree became a candelabra of a million leaf-shaped lighted candles. As a breeze stirred the leaves, the golden flames flickered. Our pathway into the village was ablaze with splendor. What Supai might be like at other seasons we would not know until later visits. But if that Indian man and maiden had attempted to leave all of this in the autumn, then they deserved to be turned into rocks.

There is a postscript to the legend. If either of the figures-turned-to-stone ever falls, then this paradise will come to an end. As we continued along this avenue of golden glory we were certain in our own minds that — if the rocks ever did fall — it would not be in autumn.

Not only was the main street lined with the gold of cottonwoods, there was color in the "street" itself. We were padding along on a wide trail of deep reddish-pink sand. Only hikers, dogs, Indian horses and mules, and villagers use this avenue of pulverized red rock. We were being provided, literally,

160

Supai's legendary rocks dominate the village.

with a red carpet approach.

There were more small houses, with saddles on the porch railings. Clothes, drying on outdoor lines, waved us welcome. Horses grazed in the fields. One rolled contentedly in the dust. A dog trotted out to sniff our packs, then escorted us in. Three other dogs, looking almost half wild, took our escort's attention, and he deserted us, just as we reached the village center, which consisted of an old lodge and a combined store and post office on one side of the wide dirt trail, and a cafe set far back on the opposite side. Beyond that we could see a small church, and a school. This was Supai.

Within minutes we were comfortably quartered in the aged lodge, where we occupied one of its three large bedrooms and enjoyed common kitchen privileges. The next-door grocery store had a few staples, principally canned goods. But also eggs and cartons of milk, all packed down on mule or horse, after having been hauled over rugged roads to Hilltop by truck. Quite understandably, the milk which we purchased was occasionally sour, but none of the eggs were ever broken. Previous guests at the lodge — not wanting to tote it out — had left their unused supplies of cereals, coffee and cocoa and tea, peanut butter and jelly. Upon our final departure, we also left what we did not use.

Throughout our Supai stay, our greatest joy in patronizing the tiny store was in visiting with the Indian women and children who were there or congregated outside, or studying the faces of the Indian men, six or eight of whom were nearly always sitting on a bench beside this combined post office and market. As we became better acquainted with them they related to us many facts and stories of interest.

"His name's Wescogame." That was our formal introduction to one aged man of the group, whose face had all the deep-carved character of the centuries-old rocks which formed the canyon walls surrounding us. One of these rocks was named, on Grand Canyon maps, Wescogame Point. This gentle Havasupai was an important man among his people.

On that first visit of ours to Supai there was a quick exploration of the rest of the village, and a "home-cooked" supper in the kitchen of our lodge. Dusk crept in quickly between these sheltering canyon walls. Tiptoeing in, also, on the heels of

Supai's "Main Street."

the dusk, came an almost complete stillness. The village was wrapped in a blanket of soft, quiet darkness. Supai had no TVs then, and no radios that we could hear.

For Helen, who was tired from our long 18-hour-day, and the hard hike down, the entire night was bathed in that silence; she was never wakened by the Armageddon which took place outside our door. A pack of dogs suddenly began going wild off toward the upper end of the village; their barking roused other dogs in the opposite direction. Howls mixed with the barking, and the noise increased, drew closer, until — so it seemed at least — all the dogs of the village were gathered just beyond our door. A canine chorus. It was an unusual occurrence, which we never heard repeated in Supai. Almost as suddenly as it had started, the melee subsided. There was peace and solitude once more.

XXVII

Miracle Falls — and Other Surprises

Legends are not to be scorned. That Indian man and his maiden who were turned to stone for attempting to leave Supai were not the only ones who have tried to escape this village — to their sorrow. The men — especially — leave frequently and often crash into disillusionment or tragedy in the outside world. The first Havasupai we had ever met — that young man whom we had passed as he was running up the trail toward Hilltop — had fared badly in his trips to the outside world.

How did we know this? He told us. He was the first person, also, whom we met and had the chance to converse with as we started out from Supai, in the sparkling brightness of an early dawn, on our journey to the three magic waterfalls.

With an injured mourning dove in his hands, he and his little brother were on the trail just ahead of us.

"The bird is hurt. I found him. You know how to fix him?"

He had recognized us and knew that we would be friendly. For the remainder of the day he and his ten-year-old brother became our companions and guides. We learned that his trips out from the village were to get alcohol, and that this was becoming his greatest problem. In future years we would aid him when he faced severe problems in the outside world. But now — for this golden day — all of us let the magic of this paradise fill our lives as it flowed around us.

It flowed — literally. Havasu Creek was the creator of much of this magic which filled the air. Its waters — impregnated with chemicals (calcium, calcium sulfate, magnesium chloride and carbonates) — are actually as turquoise blue as Navajo jewelry. Havasu means "blue-green water." There have been enchanted visitors who insist that the waters are blue even after dark, or if cupped in the hand.

The creek itself was blue and when we came to Navajo Falls — the first of the three gems — the water retained all its sparkling color as it tumbled downward.

On journeys here in later years we found Navajo Falls almost concealed by trees and undergrowth — cottonwoods, willows, box elder, hackberry, creeping wild grapevines — but on this first visit it plunged straight downward in isolated grandeur. Our camera lenses drank in the scene, and we sought locations for other shots. "No. Don't bother. Come with us."

Our self-appointed guide headed down the canyon, leaving the falls behind. Why was this? we wondered.

Within minutes we had the explanation. The answer almost stunned us. He led us to Havasu Falls.

We peered down on Havasu, first from above. We nearly lost our footing as we negotiated a steep circuitous trail, heading toward the waterfall's base. So engrossed were we in catching new views of it with each few steps that we paid no heed where we were stepping. Then we reached a vantage point where the whole spectacle spread — and rose — before us.

The views of tumbling turquoise water are but a part of the splendor. The chemicals and minerals not only give the falls their color, but they have created a background and a setting which is utterly unique. The cliffs above, underneath, and surrounding the shimmering ribbon of blue, are almost like tumbling falls themselves — except that they are formed of rock, and are frozen. They are veils of travertine, decorated with a million stalactite fingers of travertine rocks, like delicate hands silently applauding this spectacle surrounding them.

The authors' granddaughters, Krista and Jan, at Havasu Falls and pools.

And more.

That mineral coating has embraced the foliage round about — or weeds, and tree limbs, and grasses which *used* to be foliage. Now it all has been turned to delicate creations of rock-crusted vegetation. You almost swear you can see these travertine-coated grasses still waving in the breeze.

But the best is still to come; the miracle expands. The turquoise waters and the travertine deposits have fashioned a series of terraced pools at the base of Havasu Falls. Over the curved rock fringes of these pools the blue water shimmers down into the next pools of the terraces, just below. And then the next. A kaleidoscope of descending beauty. Our hike down to Supai hadn't tired us. But this view of Havasu Falls left us limp. We spent four hours absorbing it, feeling it, bathing in the pools, exploring even behind the plunging waters. We *experienced* the magic.

Mooney Falls, the third gem, may have been less magical — nothing could match Havasu — but it had other elements which made it an adventurer's utopia.

It is the highest of the Havasupai cataracts, with a drop of some 200 feet, and is surrounded with sheaths of rough-edged honeycombed rock that guard it from intruders. More than a century ago miners came here, seeking treasure. One of them, James Mooney, threw a rope down the escarpment over which the waters tumbled, and started down. He never made it alive. Other miners began a weird system of tunnels, borings, precarious miniature ladders, niched rock indentations for footholds, and cables and pegs for handholds. They made it down. That method of descent — with some modifications — is still available. All of us tried it — successfully, although scarily. Then, with our Indian friends, we went back to Havasu Falls to spend the rest of the day.

This first visit of ours to Havasu Falls was as nearly idyllic as anything we could have imagined. On a trip here two years later we began to encounter subtle changes. And on our third and fourth visits, in still later years, the place was not only over-crowded, it was becoming a "hangout" for outside characters who were marring — even destroying — the beauty. On our fourth Supai visit, the village itself had even grown to the point that it was strangely different. New buildings were in process of

The trail leading down to the tunneled passageway to Mooney Falls is a bit rough. Helen made it, and climbs back up.

Havasupai Indian at Havasu Falls.

contruction. The isolated simplicity of earlier days was disappearing.

As we reluctantly took our departure from Havasu Falls and its pools, we found that there were still three other surprises awaiting us — like frosting on the cake, or like travertine on the rocks. The first came while enroute back to the village. Our Indian friends led us, through a tangle of brush and undergrowth, to their own secret waterhole — a great deep pool which one was supposed to enter by swinging out on a rope from a high cliff — then letting go and dropping in. Our friends showed us how. Each of our granddaughters tried it — with breathtaking success. Then Francis attempted the plunge — with breathtaking suspense. He came out, unharmed.

Surprise Number Two, back in the village, resulted from the fact that a woman had broken her leg hiking down from Hilltop; it provided a dramatic lesson in how such accidents are handled. She was brought in by horse, a helicopter was summoned from Grand Canyon Village, and she was helped in. We, and many others, trained our cameras to catch the takeoff, from an open field close to the lodge and store.

No way! The blades of that chopper, as they started spinning, fanned up a fury of dust and dirt and sand that spread like a hurricane, to envelop every person and structure in sight. By the time the air cleared and visibility returned, the helicopter was off and away. In our hair, on our clothes, in our shoes, we carried reminders of that takeoff.

Our final surprise — our farewell gift of grace from this magical land of the Havasupais — came after we had climbed back up to Hilltop and were negotiating the road back to Peach Springs, through the first stretch of open country which had been alive with jackrabbits on our inbound journey.

To the left of the road we suddenly came upon the largest herd of antelope we had ever seen. Frightened by the approach of our car, they sprang into action. Closely paralleling the road, but a bit to the left, they ran in great bounding leaps ahead of our vehicle. We were neck and neck at the start, but they began gaining, try as we did to increase our speed over the rocky road.

It was easy to count them now, for they were strung out single file. Thirty-four prong-horned, white-rumped flashes of

A hiker who broke her leg is airlifted out of Supai Village.

172

beauty, bounding with elegant gracefulness, before and beside us. It was, in reality, a farewell gift of grace.

XXVIII

Notebook Journey on Rim and Trail

Think tanks are the mode these days--places set aside where cogitators can prop their feet up on desks and let their minds float free, perhaps to snag some new scientific or psychological truth.

This Grand Canyon is the big brother of all think tanks. Whether feet are propped on a log by the Rim, or slowly trodding a silent trail in the Canyon depths, thoughts float in on every breeze. These are some stray concepts which have come to us in this manner:

A God-inspired Workout Bowl

This Canyon is not only the big brother of all "think tanks," it is the parent of all health clubs, at least so far as we are concerned. Francis was a natural-born hiker; Helen was not. It was here--and in the California High Sierra--that she really learned the art of hiking.

Much of GRAND CANYON LOVE STORY was written by Francis and Helen along the trails or the Rim.

That has been her salvation. Helen's mother was bed-ridden for 20 years with crippling arthritis. The necessity of staying in absolutely top-notch physical condition for our Grand Canyon hiking has helped Helen overcome periodic bouts with that painful ailment--and also a palpitating heart.

Once, just two weeks before we were going to head for a long-planned Canyon hike, Helen had an arthritic attack so severe she could not walk from the bed to the bathroom. She gritted her teeth, she prayed (and so did Francis), she went on a careful diet, and took a few more steps each day. At the end of two weeks of care and caring, we made the rugged 20 mile Grand Canyon hike we had planned.

If a time comes when, even after teeth-gritting, either of us cannot make it, so what? All our years of having accomplished such hikes successfully have added zest, health, and wonder to our lives. For us, this Canyon has been not only a life-saver but a constant *life-giver*. Its trails are built-in "exercisers" where for years we have enjoyed God-inspired workouts in this finest of natural health spas.

* * *

These Canyon trails can provide psychological exercise as well as physical workouts. Example: The first time we laboriously ascended the Bright Angel Trail's "Corkscrew" on the ten mile climb from Phantom Ranch to the South Rim we grew weary with its interminable switchbacks. But among those twists and turns we discovered a strip of rock which, through action of water over eons of time, had been metamorphosed into a glorious polished expanse of marble beauty. It became one of our favorite Canyon sights. During our ascent of the Corkscrew the following year we eagerly anticipated that polished gem which we knew lay somewhere ahead. We came upon it, admired it, then talked at length about its subtle beauty as our ascent continued. Suddenly Helen asked, "Where are the switchbacks?" In our absorption over that natural miracle we had forgotten all about our climbing. The metamorphosed rock had metamorphosed drudgery into delight. Tedium had turned into treasure. The menacing Corkscrew had been obliterated by a mental concept.

* * *

The Canyon Rim is one of the finest places on earth to get a bird's eye view while standing on the ground.

* * *

Francis, who cut his teeth on the writings of Thoreau, is glad that Helen has taught him to saunter along the trails, rather than always being in a hurry.

Saunter, as Thoreau explains, comes from the "idle people who roved about the country, in the Middle Ages, and asked charity, under pretense of going a la Sainte Terre,"[1] to the Holy Land, till the children exclaimed, "There goes a 'Sainte-Terrer'," a Saunterer, A Holy-Lander. We have become Grand Canyon saunterers. We make no haste on the trails, but laze along, looking at every little thing, or writing in our journal, or taking pictures of some towering formations, or small flower lodged in a stone wall. We feel at home here, as the other meaning of the word saunter suggests--"sans terre," meaning having no home, but equally at home everywhere. And in a sense we are treading on a Holy Land! So why hurry--we are already there!

* * *

Most mountains are climbed from the bottom up. If you can get up Mt. Whitney, or Rainier, or even Everest, you are fairly sure of getting down. The hard part--the real challenge--comes first.

Not so Grand Canyon. Many an unaware (and unskilled) hiker has blithely made the descent to the Tonto Platform, or even to the river itself, usually in the cool of the morning.

But then! The Grand Canyon is a mountain upside down. It

has seduced you, enticed you, got you in its grasp. And now she may not let you go — at least without much more effort than you might have thought would be required.

The Grand Canyon is a mountain giant standing on its head!

* * *

A thousand-blossomed shrub is perched on the Canyon brink, each bloom and petal absorbing the grandeur below. Who knows, that plant's beauty may result as much from absorption of the view, as from nourishment sucked from the rocky soil.

* * *

In the past two years we have met half a dozen couples whose married life together began on Grand Canyon's Rim. This is not only an extension of the current desire for outdoor weddings; it clothes each such wedding in a symbolism which may be a large ingredient in its permanence.

It will surely be harder for a couple, at the first disagreement, to nurse thoughts of separation or running home to mother, if they start to think of the setting for their marriage. The very stuff of the Canyon — the endurance and permanence of those two-billion-year-old rocks — become a part of the vows.

"Do you take this woman/this man for your lawfully wedded spouse, in sickness and in health, for richer, for poorer, for better, or worse — as long as you both shall live?"

The very rocks in the Canyon's depths echo the response. "I do."

* * *

When we tell our friends that we are going to Grand Canyon again to celebrate our wedding anniversary, many of them wonder why. Our reply is that we can never get enough of it. There is so much to learn. The Canyon is an encyclopedia of history, geology, archaeology, philosophy and religion, and it will take years to understand it all. We come to celebrate our life together in a different dimension. Life is a mystery and it takes

179

years even to understand all that the Great Spirit has to reveal and teach us. The Grand Canyon is as good a yardstick as we will find. Each year our hiking has opened new visions of what life is all about, and our part in it. We find that the Canyon needs to be savored. One taste is not enough. So back to the Canyon.

* * *

The debate continues: Which Rim is better, scenically and livably — the North Rim or the South? There is no answer; it is like comparing oranges and apples. They are different.

* * *

The Grand Canyon is the love child of Mother Nature and Father Time.

* * *

Michelangelo looked at a great block of raw marble and said: "Inside that block is concealed an angel." With chisel and hammer, he began revealing his dream.

The God of the outdoors once surveyed a vast sloping plateau, which we now call the Kaibab. "Beneath that stretch of earth," he must have whispered, "is hidden a Sleeping Giant." With tools he began his work. The Sleeping Giant has been revealed.

When we look at Grand Canyon, we think of Michelangelo. The Grand Canyon is the world's masterpiece of sculpture. Thoreau put it well, in a slightly different way:

"The finest workers in stone are not copper or steel tools, but the gentle touches of air and water working at their leisure with a liberal allowance of time."

* * *

At any one of the Canyon's view points, an Eastman Kodak stockholder could smack his lips in glee, then rush to the nearest gift shop to buy more souvenirs out of the profit he anticipates

180

So many Japanese visit Grand Canyon that books and guides printed in Japanese are available at Canyon shops.

from the sale of all that film.

* * *

Spread before us is one of earth's most awesome displays of rocks.

Rocks are the ingredients of greatness.

David slew Goliath with a rock from his slingshot.

Jesus advised homebuilders to "build your house upon a rock."

Rocks are symbolic: "The Rock of Gibralter." "As solid as a rock." "Rock of Ages."

The Grand Canyon is clothed in greatness in the very nature of its ingredients. It is a 200 mile panorama of *ROCK*. It is a mile deep gash into and through the very foundations of the earth — *ROCK*. It is a ten-mile-wide rock-lover's paradise.

Every year, thousands of rockhounds gather from across the world at the tiny crossroads town of Quartsite, Arizona, southwest of Grand Canyon, to display gems and swap yarns about *rocks*. They could profitably adjourn each such annual session to the South Rim, to ponder the greatest rock collection of all.

* * *

The majority of all passengers arriving at Grand Canyon's airport are from overseas. One quarter of the park's visitors are foreigners. Japanese and German are heard, next only to English, along the South Rim. Hikers on the trails come from Europe, Africa, Australia, Asia, and the Americas. Grand Canyon is a magnet for the people of the world.

And now it has become more than that. In the open air patio of the visitor center a large metal plaque on a native rock tells the story. The Canyon is no longer just American. It has been designated as a world heritage site. The plaque reads:

THROUGH THE COLLECTIVE RECOGNITION OF THE COMMUNITY OF NATIONS EXPRESSED WITHIN THE PRINCIPLES OF THE CONVENTION CONCERNING THE PROTECTION OF THE WORLD CULTURAL AND NATURAL HERITAGE GRAND

CANYON NATIONAL PARK HAS BEEN DESIGNATED
A WORLD HERITAGE SITE AND JOINS A SELECT
LIST OF PROTECTED AREAS AROUND THE WORLD
WHOSE OUTSTANDING NATURAL AND CULTURAL
RESOURCES FORM THE COMMON INHERITANCE
OF ALL MANKIND

OCTOBER 26, 1979

* * *

Fred Harvey — and El Tovar, Bright Angel, and the other South Rim lodges operated by the company he originally formed — had an important role in the lore of Grand Canyon.

Fred Harvey migrated from England in 1850 and began his career as a dishwasher in a New York restaurant. Later he became a railroad passenger agent and mail clerk. Food and food service along the railways were bad; he thought he could do better, and sought permission from the Santa Fe to open eating places along their route. These Harvey Houses expanded. "Harvey Girl" waitresses by the hundreds were brought West to serve the tasty Harvey meals. Judy Garland took the part of one of these girls in a 1949 movie. Will Rogers said that Fred Harvey "kept the West in food and wives."

The Santa Fe extended a branch rail line to Grand Canyon in 1901; the Harvey Company came soon after. El Tovar Hotel was built at a cost of $250,000, just one-twentieth the cost of a remodeling job completed there in 1983.

In 1905, the Harvey Company built the Hopi House, and hired Indian craftsmen to demonstrate their skills for tourists. The original Fred Harvey, who died in 1901, is said never to have seen Grand Canyon. But "Fred Harvey" has bedded down Canyon tourists, provided mule transportation to the Canyon's depths, and prepared food for millions, in the more than three-quarters of a century that the company has been the principal Grand Canyon host.

* * *

The Bright Angel Trail provides a symphony of sounds: the

Grand Canyon is for the enjoyment and uplift of all the world.

184

fragile, plaintive fluting of woodwind notes by unnamed birds, or the canyon wren trilling up and down the scale, like a Lily Pons. The cliff swallows, darting swiftly, chasing like children, gleefully, dipping and twittering, cutting the air, making their impression on this ancient handiwork of nature. People who have gotten acquainted as they pass and repass along the trail, chatting like old friends, as they gather at Indian Gardens, or rest along the way. Lasting friendships are begun. Deep, deep breathing of both mules and hikers as they ascend Jacob's Ladder, that set of tortuous zigzags. And finally the hurrahs of climbers as they top out on the South Rim. The sights and sounds leave one breathless.

* * *

Geologically, the changes at Grand Canyon are imperceptible over the course of 50 years. The chasm has grown perhaps half an inch wider and a quarter of an inch deeper in the last half century. Economically, the changes in the prices for food and facilities in that same 50 years have been titanic. An El Tovar room today may cost $60 or $70. According to our 1940 Works Progress Administration Arizona guidebook, a room — along with three meals — at El Tovar totaled $4.25. Bright Angel Lodge rooms, in 1940, were $1.25 a day, breakfasts 50 cents up, and dinners 85 cents up. A night at Phantom Ranch, including meals, went at $6.00. An all-expense overnight Phantom Ranch mule trip was $18.00. All of which demonstrates that the Grand Canyon is just keeping up with the times.

* * *

Mystery. That is our feeling as we stand at the ruins of the Anasazi Indian pueblo of Tusayan, a short distance back in the forest from the Canyon's South Rim. Probably no more than 30 of these early inhabitants dwelt here. To the south, their view took in the San Francisco Peaks where, in all probability, they witnessed the volcanic eruptions which lit the skies there during the twelfth century. The deep gorge of Grand Canyon, a moment's walk to the north, was their constant companion.

𐄂𐄂𐄂

Grand Canyon National Park

Season: South Rim, open all year; North Rim, June 1-Sept. 30, or later if roads are clear.
Administrative Offices: South Rim, Grand Canyon Village; North Rim, 11 miles south of entrance gate, address Kaibab Forest.
Admission: $1 entrance fee for automobile, motorcycle, or trailer.
Transportation: (South Rim) Santa Fe Ry., train or bus from Williams. (North Rim) busses of. Utah Parks Co., subsidiary of Union Pacific R.R. from Jacob Lake. Independent busses connect with Utah Parks busses at Jacob Lake.
South Rim Sightseeing Trips: West Rim Drive, $3. East Rim Drive, $6., combined $7. All-expense overnight mule trip to Phantom Ranch, $18. All-expense 3-day mule trip to Phantom Ranch and Ribbon Falls, $28. Cross-canyon, 2-day all-expense mule trip, $30. Hermit Basin and Dripping Springs 1-day all-expense horse trip, $6. Supai motor-pony trip: private cars may be driven to Hilltop; taxi service, $21 a person round trip; Indian pony, Hilltop to Supai, round trip, $5. Accommodations at Supai limited, telephone for reservations; bed, $1.50, meals, 75¢ each, ponies, $1.50 a day. Also independent camping trips. Saddle horses: 2-hour trips in charge of guide, $1.50 a person. Horses 2 hours, $1.50, day, $5. Special guide, full day, $5. Tuba City and Moenkopi 1-day all-expense automobile trip, $12 a person. Also chartered automobiles.
North Rim Sightseeing Trips: from Grand Canyon Lodge to Cape Royal and Point Imperial, $3 a person; from Grand Canyon Lodge to Point Sublime, 3 person minimum, $5 a person.
North Rim Trail Trips: 1-day all-expense mule trip to Roaring Springs, $7 a person; 2-day all-expense mule trip to Phantom Ranch, $20 a person; 2-day cross-canyon mule trip (*see South Rim*). Saddle horses: 2-hour trips with guide, $1.50 a person. Saddle horses without guide 2 hours, $1.50, half-day, $3. Guide, half-day $3, full day, $5. Also camping trips.
Airplane Service: Grand Canyon Airlines, Inc., airport near each rim, 90-mile flights, including 60 miles of Grand Canyon, 2 person minimum, $8.50 each; cross-canyon flight, 2 person minimum, 1 way, $10 each; round trip, indefinite stopover, $15 each. Also charter flights.
Accommodations: South Rim: El Tovar Hotel, Am. plan, from $4.25 a day. Bright Angel Lodge, E. plan, from $1.50 a day; breakfast, 50¢ up, luncheon, 75¢ up, dinners, 85¢ up. Public camp, $1.25 and $1.75 a day; housekeeping cabins, $2.25 a day, bedding extra. Phantom Ranch, bottom of canyon, Am. plan, $6 a day. Free camp site with wood and water at auto camp and Desert View. Rowe's Well cabins, $1.25 and $2.50. North Rim: Grand Canyon Lodge, E. plan, rooms from $2.25. Breakfast and luncheon, $1, dinner, $1.25. Housekeeping cabins, $2 to $4.50. A few 2-cot tents, $1.70. Free camp sites with water and fuel. Cafeteria at auto camp; breakfast, 75¢, luncheon, 75¢, dinner, 90¢.
Climate: South Rim: Air dry, evenings cool, summers hot with occasional thunder showers. Snow in winter. Lower canyon usually 20° warmer than plateaus. North Rim: June and Sept. evenings chilly, July and August warm, with frequent thunder showers. Deep snow during winter.
Clothing and Equipment: Warm clothing in winter; warm wraps for evening in summer; long sleeved shirt, sun hat, and boots for trails. Riding clothes and shade hats rented at all hotels.

In 1940, prices at Grand Canyon were low, as shown by this page from a W.P.A. Arizona Guidebook.

As one views the Canyon today it is important to realize that this was home to some of our original Americans.

* * *

Few things about Grand Canyon are conventional. One aspect of it is so nonconformist and filled with mystery that it is officially designated "The Great Unconformity." At South Rim's Yavapai Museum this can be observed, as a ranger-geologist explains it.

Looking across to the North Rim you see Paleozoic layers resting directly on the Vishnu schist — that hardest layer of the Canyon, through which the river flows. But you also see other places where a layer of Hakatai shale intervenes between these two. What caused this Hakatai layer — in some places — to disappear completely? This layer, perhaps five hundred million years old, has vanished.

The explanations are somewhat uncertain and tentative. Where has that half-billion-year-old layer gone? That's a mighty gap! That's a mystery.

Once you've seen this Unconformity, you can never unsee it — it makes you ponder. It makes you say, "How great that there are still mysteries to confound us!"

XXIX

Color It Gold, Again!

1978

Our second hike to the Grand Canyon village of the Havasupais, on May 1 of 1977, really started something.

We take a trip, somewhere in the world, on every wedding anniversary. May 1, 1977, was our 49th anniversary. Although we had been down to Supai before — probably *because* we had been there before — we decided that was the spot for the celebration of our 49th.

One year later, of course, came our 50th. That was the big one. Where to go?

The choice was not hard to make. Phantom Ranch, despite an earlier disappointment, was a favorite spot with us. The round trip hike from South Rim to Phantom would be a 50th anniversary challenge, a real celebration.

That hike definitely established the trend. We have been making some kind of a Grand Canyon hike every anniversary since.

The experience on our 50th was so golden that, the day we returned home, we dashed off a descriptive letter to our closest friends. The result caught the immediacy of that anniversary adventure.

May we assume that you are numbered among our special friends? If so, we invite you to read the letter, just as we dashed it off.

Dear Friends:

A 50th wedding anniversary, we discovered, is symbolically similar to the Grand Canyon, where we spent ours in an exciting hiking adventure. This important milestone has given us a new breadth of vision, and a new depth of experience, which we just did not have before. Like the Canyon, we have been subjected to maturing forces. Grand Canyons and 50th anniversaries both are charged with elements of depth and vision, and experiences of climbing.

At 5 a.m. on May 1, we looked out the window of the cabin at Bright Angel Lodge, on the South Rim, and saw sprinklings of snow on cars and rooftops. This seemed no hazard so we ate a small breakfast, packed, and at 6:10 a.m. stepped out the door to start our hike down to Phantom Ranch on the Colorado River.

A blizzard struck us in the face. Snow swirls filled the air, the ground was white, and the wind was whipping cold. Leaving our gear in the cabin, we at once went up to the lobby to reconsider plans.

Yes, we could cancel our Phantom Ranch reservations if we desired. It would be 7 o'clock before a decision would be made as to whether the mule passengers would be making the journey down.

We debated procedures as the blizzard grew worse. Our plans called for descending on the steep but shorter Kaibab Trail, and returning on the Bright Angel Trail. The Kaibab, we were told, would be just too dangerous under conditions of snow and wind and mud. So we donned heavy ponchos, with parka-like caps, used socks for mittens (for we had not dreamed we would need these), got a German tourist to snap our picture at the head of Bright Angel Trail, and started down at 7:40 a.m.

MUD. SNOW. GOO. WIND. Slippery red clay quagmires. COLD! This wasn't exactly what we had visioned as

Helen, on their 50th wedding anniversary, tries to avoid the mud.

our 50th wedding celebration. Sometimes the trail was nothing but continuous puddles of red water, which we had to jump across. Sometimes it was sloughs of crimson slush. When rocks were mud-covered they were slippery on the switchbacks; at such times, we had to take each step with caution befitting a newly wedded bride, rather than 50 year veterans.

The mule trips had not been cancelled. "It would take a flood or an avalanche," the wrangler said, "to cancel those." The mule train, with luggage and supplies, approached us from behind and according to trail rules we stood on the outside of the trail to assist their passage. "Better stand on the inside," motioned the wrangler to us. "Less chance of a mule brushing you off." In a few minutes, the mule train with the guests, also heading for Phantom Ranch, came by.

The clay mud had been bad before but the hooves of 20 mules turned it into a churned-up unending series of switchback mud pies. In places, the mule tracks showed that even those surefooted animals had occasionally slipped and slid. And twice we saw where deer had slipped!

By 9:30 a.m. we began to meet hikers coming up from their overnight stay at Indian Gardens — about halfway to the Ranch — where it had rained instead of snowed. At every meeting the question from them and from us was almost always, "How's the mud ahead?" A trail co-maraderie soon developed, and before the day was over we had exchanged greetings with hikers from the Swiss Alps, from Germany, Norway, Sweden, Belgium, Canada, and France, as well as a dozen American states.

By the one-and-a-half mile rest shelter the storm had ceased, but the next mile and one-half — to the second shelter and water — was the worst of the day for slippery mud and ooziness. Then a ray of sunshine broke the clouds, and Indian Gardens was a mile-and-a-half away.

Lest you think the trail itself is all there is to this journey, we want to say that everyone is moved to exclaim again and again at the vastness of the canyons, the walls of solid rock, the almost overpowering bigness of everything.

Violent *FLASH FLOODS* sometimes occur during summer thunderstorms. Water collects along walls of this side canyon and funnels thru this narrow gorge. Resulting floodwaters may reach a depth of several feet and carry a staggering load of silt, sand, debris and even large boulders.

The authors hope a flash flood doesn't arrive today.

193

It is something one has to experience, to comprehend the feeling of height, depth, and breadth of it all . . . the colors of the escarpments, the bird calls, and the fragrances of unknown shrubbery . . . it creates its own atmosphere. We said so many times during the day, "O God, how wonderful are thy works in this land. It fills our hearts and souls with its wonder, and we thank you for it." Helen often went singing "Jesus hold my hand as I walk this trail, Jesus hold my hand as I walk this trail, for I don't want to walk this trail in vain." Around each switchback was a different alluring vista of grandeur. We were slipping from life-zone to life-zone, growing warmer and warmer as we headed into Indian Gardens.

Almost suddenly, mysteriously, a flower garden began spreading before and around us. This was more like the storybook version we had dreamed of. No 50th anniversary celebration had ever had such a bouquet of extravagant beauty as was spread about us here. Helen was in seventh heaven. One special white flowering, she called her Wedding Bouquet!

On into Indian Gardens we were thrilled at the number and variety of flowers. Literally millions of Mariposa lilies lifted their dainty cups. There were plentiful Indian paintbrush, graceful mallow, yellow encelia, Spanish daggers, yuccas, daisies, larkspur, and many more we couldn't name. It was a garden beyond compare, not even overshadowed by the beauty of the Canyon itself. It stood a testament to its own loveliness.

We ate a handful of trailmix and some dried fruit here, and took advantage of their running water and facilities. It was delightful sitting under great cottonwood trees for our rest stop. Many persons only come this far, often carrying heavy packs and camping out. They come down quite easily, but the upward climb is a wearying one. Hard!

From Indian Gardens down to the Colorado River there were more torturous switchbacks but now the trail was nearly dry. Streams wound beside us which we often had to cross and recross by leaping from stone to stone.

On one precarious turn we met a friendly park ranger.

We told him this was our 50th anniversary, and that we were sure we would make it down, but that coming out might be a different story. "If you've come this far, you can surely make it out," he encouraged us. "Just take your time. If you have any trouble going out tell the ranger at Indian Gardens. He'll be able to help you."

This was encouragement which we needed. Each time we entered a new canyon we said, "The Colorado River will be here." But no. This was the most interminable part of the trek. Seemingly the river never would appear! Canyon after canyon, great up-lifting of the rocks in folds, if you can imagine that, gave a strange feeling of living in another age and time. When we finally reached the river Helen was really tired. The 1.7 miles on into Phantom Ranch we supposed would be flat and easy going. Instead it was up one rock escarpment, then down another, with some switchbacks thrown in for good measure. When at last it did level out, right close to the river itself, this trail became one continuous churned-up sandpile — some of the hardest hiking of the day.

We saw three river boats shooting the rapids as we crossed the narrow suspension bridge, the one that the hikers use. It was a bit scary for Helen, as the bridge gave her a dizzy feeling, and the river was wide and churning white — ominously deep — all visible through the open grillwork underfoot.

At 3:50 p.m. we were crossing Bright Angel Creek, now a roaring river, and soon we were at our beautiful cottage close to its sound. Phantom Ranch was no longer a phantom. We loved it, under green bowers of cottonwoods, with cool streams and frog ponds, which supplied us with their music as we napped.

Our hearty dinner was at 6:00 p.m., and all the guests gathered at the sound of a cowbell, which resounded through the canyon. It was a friendly group at our table. People from Pittsburg, Chicago, Ontario, California, Israel, and Germany. The man in charge of the dining room said it was the manager's birthday, and suggested that we all sing happy birthday when he came out, which we did — lustily!

Francis can't avoid the deep sand of the River Trail.

Then the man from Ontario said it was his birthday too, so we repeated the song; it was all very gala.

Then Francis got up and said, "In a small Michigan town, on May 1, 1928, Helen and I were married at 7 a.m., so that we could get an early start on our honeymoon to Kentucky. We have been traveling and adventuring ever since, and today is our 50th wedding anniversary. To celebrate it we hiked down in the snow and mud from the South Rim to Phantom Ranch. We hope to hike out tomorrow. I want to propose a toast to Helen Line, the most wonderful girl in the world."

The kitchen crew had come in. They--and the more than 50 guests--really applauded. Everyone wished us the best and congratulated us. Even some boy scouts came up afterwards to shake our hands and wish us happiness. We shall cherish these memories the rest of our lives.

After our dinner we went out under the stars on the banks of Bright Angel Creek and recited our marriage vows to each other, adding some new concepts to make them even more meaningful.

It was a precious moment in this most exciting trip. We both said there is something so special about 50 years of togetherness that just can't be measured. It's a part of the great intangibles of living. We felt it, perhaps more fully, due to our trip through the spaces of this marvelous Grand Canyon, where we had literally dropped through ages of time, through two billion years. Our lives had unrolled as we slipped down that trail. It is something like seeing a movie of your life run backward. The memories crowd in and you measure them against the agelessness of the Canyon. It's quite an experience and one we would wish for any couple who wants to evaluate their lives.

After a 6:30 breakfast next morning we left Phantom Ranch at 7:05. Helen had recovered her zip and set a fast pace for us, making Francis really strain to keep up with her. It was exhilarating in the cool of the morning. At one point on the switchbacks winding up out of the Colorado gorge we passed a wall of rose-colored marble, rough but beautiful, and then came to a place where water and sand and silt had poured over it for centuries — until nature had worn it down. It was a metamorphosed bedrock, solid rough marble changed by action of nature. That thrilled us. We like the idea of being metamorphosed — changed into something new and wonderful. This dry waterfall was a ribbon of soft-looking silk, rose and white, flowing down that great canyon wall. We asked ourselves — if rough marble can be metamorphosed why not persons, until they become more Christlike? Change is certainly one of the main features of this mighty Grand Canyon. Who knows what it will be in the future centuries?

We made it to the top of the switchbacks and on to Indian Gardens before the mules appeared, and everyone cheered us as they went by. At the Gardens stop one of the men said, "I hope I have your vitality when I celebrate my 50th wedding anniversary," and a man in his 30's spoke up, "I wish I had their vitality now!"

We all left Indian Gardens together, and began passing many others coming down. A group of 30 six-and-eight-year-old children from a Tempe school were coming as far as Indian Gardens — their first trip to the Canyon. A photographer from PEOPLE MAGAZINE was along to take their pictures. They were brave little folks.

We began to see the Grand Canyon as a *blending bowl,* without an age differential, or racial barrier, or social wall separating anyone. There had been people of all races and colors on this trail. We especially felt drawn to a young black man from Guinea, West Africa, who had been studying in France, and who was taking a bus tour of the USA before returning to Guinea to teach. He had seen movies of the Canyon in school in Africa, and had always yearned to visit it. We asked him what his impressions of it were. "Oh," he said, "Its immensities are incomprehensible." We shared some of our trailmix with him and took his name and address with the hope that someday our paths will cross again.

At each rest place on the way out we met fine hikers, and interesting conversations took place between peoples

This man whom the Lines met had come all the way from Africa to see the Canyon, because he had studied about it in school.

from all over the world. It was an enriching episode of the adventure.

Closer to the top we passed another park ranger coming down, and he asked us, "Are you the couple who are celebrating. their 50th anniversary?" We said we were, and wondered how he knew. "Why, it's all over the Canyon. You're a wonder to everyone on this trail. They all wish they had your stamina, and the joy you have in doing it." We passed a girl from Eugene, Oregon, who insisted on taking our picture, with us kissing. She wanted it as a keepsake of a happy couple.

At 2:45 p.m. we ate our last sandwich which the Ranch had given us. With only a mile and one-half yet to go we started out, looking upward at each switchback, estimating which century we were passing through. Each layer of this Canyon was put down in a different period, with the river cutting downward at the same speed that the Canyon was pushed upward. The combination of these forces helped create this great gash in the earth. One woman on the trail said, "It's quite a ditch, isn't it?" We talked with a man from Bavaria, met more Swiss Alpine hikers — all persons of interest and worth.

Nearing the last mile we caught up with a couple of young fellows who were exhausted with carrying their heavy packs. They had run out of food and were weak, so we shared our trailmix with them, and they were grateful. We find that trailmix is one of the best picker-ups there is. That and raisins and a few dried fruits are our main foods while hiking.

With the weather well nigh perfect we topped out on the South Rim nine hours and 40 minutes after leaving Phantom Ranch. Helen came in great, so Francis said, but she made quick work getting out of her hiking shoes and unwinding all the tape she'd put around each of her toes to protect them. She didn't get one blister by using this system. All we could say was — *we made it! Thank God.* Nearly 20 miles, with almost a 5000 foot altitude gain — a hundred feet for every year we'd been married.

A 50th anniversary hike in the Grand Canyon, we

discovered, is a sacred adventure in time and space. *We recommend it!*

"Wide Horizons," always.

Francis & Helen

The Lines top out after their 50th wedding anniversary hiking adventure.

XXX

The Cemetery
Is a History Book[1]

The 1980s

Some Grand Canyon visitors find that their greatest exhilaration comes at Grandview Point. Others go into the Canyon's hidden depths for solace and satisfaction. Among those who love the Canyon best, Point Sublime is often the chosen spot for seeking uplift. All of these places electrify the spirit.

One other Grand Canyon location can do this also. In one sense, if the visitor carries his imagination and his empathies with him, it is the place which inspires most. It is Grand Canyon's Pioneer Cemetery, just west of the Shrine of the Ages, not far from the visitor center on South Rim.

Until the 1980s we had never known that this place existed. Then, just before leaving the park on one of our annual anniversary trips, we paid a quick visit, and were stirred. We did some research and some reading, and made a trip back from California to become thoroughly acquainted with this tiny spot, just a few acres in a colossal national park and Canyon which embraces nearly two thousand square miles. This is one of three

203

places at Grand Canyon which lift the curtain to help reveal its total human story.

The first is Tusayan Ruin; there one feels the presence of those original inhabitants — the native Americans — who came here, lived here, laughed and loved here, then disappeared. The Anazasis were the first humans who left a record at the Canyon.

At Moran Point, one looks into the mists and remembers that near here was the first place where non-Indians discovered Grand Canyon. The Spanish explorers saw it, tried to conquer it, and — failing to effect a crossing — left and went their ways.

The native Americans dwelt here in the 1100s and 1200s A.D. The Spaniards first came in 1540. Then within the last century other men and women, courageous trailblazers, pioneers, and ordinary citizens, have left their marks and added pages to the Canyon's human history. Their stories, their imprints, the legacies and legends of many of these are revealed — for those whose imaginations are graphic — in the small plots of earth and simple wood or stone markers, in Grand Canyon's Pioneer Cemetery.

John Hance's grave comes first, and well it should. Just 150 feet inside the cemetery gate, a slender, rough, irregularly shaped four-foot-high slab of sandstone announces: "Captain John Hance, first locator in Grand Canyon. Arizona pioneer. Trail builder and guide. Died January 8, 1919. Aged 80 years."

Hance was a loveable person, a true "character" of the early day West, who came to Grand Canyon on a prospecting reconnoiter in 1883. He loved the place, built a cabin near Grandview Point, and became the Canyon's first white settler. His name was given to the old and the new Hance Trails. He accommodated guests at his cabin and became a guide for trips into the Canyon.

Hance was a storyteller in the most exalted sense — a yarn-spinning prevaricator. Our friend, the late travel-lecturer Burton Holmes, related many tall tales about the Canyon that John Hance spun, in which it was impossible to separate fact from fancy.

Hance sold his Grandview ranch holdings but the subsequent hotel there was put out of business when the Sante Fe put its rail spur through to the spot where El Tovar was built. Hance's

One who steps through the entrance of Pioneer Cemetery begins to experience the human history of Grand Canyon.

205

location excelled, in sweep and view, the vista obtained from present El Tovar.

When a Grand Canyon post office was established, at the old Hance ranch, John Hance became the first postmaster. He was "first" in many respects.

William Bass, a Canyon pioneer who arrived not long after Hance, and who left even more lasting marks than the latter, is not buried in the Pioneer Cemetery. When he died, in 1933, his ashes, as he requested, were scattered by airplane over the Canyon's Holy Grail Temple, known as "Bass Tomb." A large monument to him has been erected in the cemetery, by Arizona's governor, Bruce Babbitt.

But Mrs. Bass, whose grave is in the cemetery, was a pioneer with credentials all her own. William Bass, in 1892, was guiding occasional visitors on horseback forays into Havasu Canyon, land of the Havasupais. One such visitor was Ada Diefendorf, a music teacher from New York state, who had graduated from the Boston Conservatory of Music. William played the violin; there was a common ground of interest. Two years later they were married, Mrs. Bass moved to Bass Camp near Havasupai Point, and made history. The plaque on her gravestone sums it up briefly: "Ada Lenore Diefendorf Bass, Aug. 29, 1869. May 5, 1951. Grand Canyon Pioneer, 1890. 1st white woman to raise a family on rim of Grand Canyon."

The Bass's had four children. When Mrs. Bass went "shopping," it meant an overnight 73 mile journey to Ashfork. She has said that she has prepared a meal, or slept, under every tree on the route.

A permanent water supply did not exist at Bass Camp. Nor even at Ashfork. That was one of the two places where Francis and his brother, in 1923, had to buy water; it was hauled in by the Santa Fe. When Mrs. Bass did her laundry, she sometimes had to make the three day hike down into the Canyon's depths to the Colorado River. A woman like that deserves a resting place in Grand Canyon's pioneer burial ground.

So, too, do Emery and Ellsworth Kolb. When Emery died, in 1976, at the age of 95, it marked the end of an era in Grand Canyon's human history. The Kolb studio and home, where he had lived for much of his life, still stands, clinging to the very edge of the Rim just at the head of Bright Angel Trail. There, in 1923, Francis had heard him narrate the filmed story of the Kolb brothers' running of the Colorado River in 1911. Helen and Francis had heard the same lecture several times in later years.

His marker, to the left as one enters the cemetery, reads: "Photographer, Artist, Explorer, Lecturer, A hard worker and doer of many things."

Beside him is the grave and marker of his wife: "Blanche M. Kolb, Canyon resident for 55 years. Illustrious beloved wife and mother."

Less than a hundred feet from the grave of his brother, is the grave and marker reading: "Ellsworth L. Kolb, Jan. 4, 1872, Jan. 9, 1960. Photographer, Explorer, Author."

It is a bit less easy to say that the Hon. Ralph H. Cameron deserves a burial spot at Grand Canyon, but perhaps, with death, there should be forgiveness for aberrations. Ralph Cameron, who died in Washington, D.C. in 1955, was a delegate there from the Arizona territory, from 1909 to 1912; he obtained statehood for Arizona in 1912, and he was Arizona's United States Senator from 1921 to 1927. His marker reads: "Arizona can never forget him."

That is the point. Around Grand Canyon he is remembered, not so much for his beneficent achievements, as for the fact that he took mining claims on many of the South Rims's vital areas, including the Bright Angel Trail, for the purpose of controlling them; he put money ahead of vision, and stood in the way of the park's development. But he *is* remembered.

So too are the victims of what was, at the time of its occurrence, one of the nation's worst aviation disasters. Both flying eastward, with nearly perfect visibility, two great passenger planes collided over Grand Canyon, in 1956, and fell to earth out beyond Desert View, killing all 128 passengers aboard the two planes. A large granite marker stands in Pioneer Cemetery to their memory.

There are war memorials, too, including the Spanish-American conflict. A single large marker memorializes three Grand Canyon boys who gave their lives in World War I, and five in World War II. One of these latter was a Hopi Indian.

Half a dozen gravestones will cling permanently in our

Emery Kolb's death, at age 95, ended an era in Grand Canyon's human history. His wife is buried beside him, and his brother Ellsworth's grave is close by.

memories because of the poetic visionary idealism of the inscriptions. One of these was the marker for Gunnar Widforss. On the North Rim we had done some hiking on the Widforss Trail, named after this Swedish artist who came to the United States in 1905 and 1921 and who, after seeing the American West on the latter trip, never returned to Europe. He became an American citizen. He started painting in the national parks. He met the director of all the parks, Stephen Mather. (Francis also had the great privilege of meeting Mather in Yellowstone Park in 1925). Mather became Widforss' patron and this artist — who loved Grand Canyon best of all the parks — transferred much of its beauty to canvas.

The Widforss marker is small — a dark bronze plaque set in a rough lichen-covered Canyon rock. The sentiment on the marker is large.

"Bury this man there? Here, here's his place, where meteors shoot, clouds form Lofty designs must close in like effects Loftily lying Leave him still loftier than the world suspects Living and dying."

John H. Maxson, 1906-1966, a scientist who once worked at the Canyon, is one of the few persons buried in the Pioneer Cemetery who did not fulfill the residential requirement of having lived here long enough. His simple marker reads: "Full enjoyment of this unique natural heritage is derived not only from its appeal to the human senses but also from its understanding by the human mind."

We saw the graves of two former superintendents of Grand Canyon National Park, M. R. Tillotson and John S. McLaughlin, and the still unmarked plot of Merle Stitt, who passed away just after retiring in 1980.

Of deepest human interest, perhaps, were the resting places of simple, unheralded men and women who had loved the Canyon, and served it well. We spent half a day hunting up isolated or inconspicuous graves, and recording the illuminating (and occasionally difficult to read) markers. Each of these revealed a life that had come in loving contact with this Canyon.

Charles E. Dunn, 1885-1957. Range Rider, Grand Canyon Trails Guide. Driver of the Grand Canyon-Williams Stage. "He left something of himself with everyone he met."

John T. Smith. 1928-1978 . . . "He loved animals and the outdoors, so when he came to Grand Canyon June 1950, he found home. John started as a trailguide, then a packer, and the last thirteen years as a trail foreman.

"John was a wonderful and loving husband and father. With his kind words and a pat on our heads, we knew everything was going to be alright."

One of the longest epitaphs was for Kenneth Carmel Patrick, 1933-1973.

An inscription in bronze, of over two hundred words, details a dozen episodes in the varied life of this park ranger, relating that he always returned to the country he loved, and concluding: "then on that summer dawn in silent fog, not far away, he disturbed a deer poacher's team and they just shot him. May the memory of his devotion to all people and to that fine country of our national parks and of the splendor of his soul inspire and remain with us."

The poaching episode occurred, not at Grand Canyon, but at another national park where he served — Point Reyes National Seashore, California.

And, finally, the simplest inscription of all, which in eleven letters conveys a vivid picture of a romantic period in the human story of Grand Canyon. On the weathered bronze foot-square marker to Elsie Worden, with the dates April 19, 1908-May 9, 1945, we read the three words which gave her claim to a place in the human history of Grand Canyon and the West.

"A HARVEY GIRL"

XXXI

"The Great Unknown"

We have endeavored to explore Grand Canyon, not alone physically, but intellectually, aesthetically, and spiritually as well.

Searching out, in our reading, rare descriptive or otherwise revealing passages about the Canyon has made us the recipients of rich treasure.

What exclamation leaped from the lips of the first Spanish explorer who looked down into what would one day be named "Grand Canyon" we shall never know, although one member of the Spanish expedition is reported to have said that some of the Canyon rocks were bigger than the great tower of Seville in Spain.[1] But succeeding explorers, adventurers, VIP visitors, and ordinary lay persons have painted Grand Canyon word pictures — both brief and long — which rival the oil canvases of master artists.

"We are now ready to start on our way down the Great Unknown."[2] That was the 13-word diary entry of Major John Wesley Powell as he and his fellow explorers prepared to enter the Canyon by boat, in 1869.

"There must be few other equally accessible places on earth where it is possible to look into areas never actually explored by man." — Joseph Wood Krutch. Francis has a look.

Well over a century later, parts of the Canyon are still unknown. Joseph Wood Krutch, in a couple of dozen words, conveys its paradoxical qualities of present-day availability, yet eternal wildness. "There must be few other equally accessible places on earth where it is possible to look into areas never actually explored by man."

John Burroughs said of the Canyon, "To rave over it, or to pour into it a torrent of superlatives, is of little avail."[3]

But, Burroughs notwithstanding, superlatives crept into nearly every Grand Canyon description, whether penned by professional prose writers, explorers, engineers, soldiers, or poets.

"The most splendid exposure of stratified rock that there is in the world." Those weren't the words of some visionary bard, but of a scientist who did studies in the Canyon — the geologist Dr. John Strong Newberry, back in 1857. He was with the party of Joseph Christmas Ives, an army lieutenant sent out by the War Department to find out to what extent the Colorado River was navigable by steamboat. The Canyon descriptions by Ives, the military man, were as colorful as the scientists:

"The extent and magnitude of the system of canyons is astounding. The plateau is cut into shreds by these gigantic chasms, and resembles a vast ruin. Belts of country miles in width have been swept away, leaving only isolated mountains standing in the gap. Fissures so profound that the eye cannot penetrate their depths are separated by walls whose thickness one can almost span, and slender spires that seem to be tottering upon their bases shoot up thousands of feet from the vaults below."[4]

Ives' reputation for visionary acumen would have fared far better if he had been satisfied with those descriptive remarks. Referring to the lower Colorado — the land below the Canyon — he wrote in his report:

"The region is, of course, altogether valueless. It can be approached only from the south, and after entering it there is nothing to do but leave. Ours has been the first, and will doubtless be the last, party of whites to visit this profitless locality. It seems intended by nature that the Colorado river, along the greater portion of its lonely and majestic way, shall be forever unvisited and undisturbed."[5]

213

Another army lieutenant, George M. Wheeler, who made geographical surveys in the lower Grand Canyon in 1871, envisioned its grandeur in much the way as had Lieutenant Ives. But Wheeler's vision extended into the future in a way far different. He wrote:

"These stupendous specimens of extended rock-carving . . . stand without a rival upon the face of the globe . . . and will, as circumstances of transportation permit, attract the denizens of all quarters of the world . . ."[6]

From all quarters of the globe they have come, tourists from Germany and Japan, hikers from Norway and Switzerland and the Tyrol, youth groups from Canada and Australia, writers from England, poets from France, just plain people from everywhere. The Canyon is a mighty magnet, drawing devotees from across the world.

They come for all reasons. W. E. Garrett of the National Geographic Magazine described one such reason. He called the Canyon the place "Where you can take your soul for a long walk — slowly."[7]

Joaquin Miller injected a colorful — at least a rose-tinted — twist to his description: "It is old, old, this Grand Canyon, and yet so new it seems almost to smell of paint — red paint, pink, scarlet . . . every shade and hue of red, as far as the eye can compass. It is a scene of death-like silence, a dead land of red, a burning world."[8]

In attempting to write about the Canyon, humorist Irvin S. Cobb declared: "Nearly everybody, on taking a first look at the Grand Canyon, comes right out and admits its wonders are absolutely indescribable, and then proceeds to write anywhere from two thousand to fifty thousand words giving the full details."[9]

John McCutcheon was not primarily a writer, but a pen and ink artist, who portrayed Grand Canyon in cartoons. He did, however, come up with an article which contained some advice to Canyon-bound writers which is worth pondering. He said: "In describing the Grand Canyon, one should go into a course of literary training and gradually work up to it. He should start off on the Bay of Naples, do that until he has perfected it, then tackle the sunset on the domes and minarets of Stamboul and work on

"Where you can take your soul for a long walk — slowly." — W. E. Garrett. Helen takes such a walk.

215

that until he can do it in bogie. Then sunrise on Mount Rigi, the Vale of Kashmir, and other star attractions of nature . . . When a writer has tackled everything in the line of fancy descriptive writing, he crowns his life work with a pen picture of the Grand Canyon — called by some: 'The Greatest Show on Earth.' For descriptions of the Canyon, see other writers.''[10]

We are going to do just that. Other writers — dozens, scores, hundreds of them — have come up with such varied descriptions of this greatest show on earth that it is profitable to pursue these further. The Canyon, we have concluded, is like the elephant described by the blind men. One blind man felt its trunk, another an ear, another its tail, and experienced only miniscule fractions of the elephant's totality. We are all partially blind when viewing the Canyon, or at least our vision is incapable of encompassing its elephantine totality. It is literally, figuratively, aesthetically, and geographically impossible ever to experience it all. En masse, however, we all try, as we shall see further in the following chapter.

216

XXXII

"Imagine . . . Imagine . . . Imagine"

One of the greatest compliments ever bestowed on the Grand Canyon, in our opinion, came from an Englishman, J. B. Priestley, who wrote: "I have heard rumors of visitors who were disappointed. The same people will be disappointed at the Day of Judgment. In fact, the Grand Canyon is a sort of landscape Day of Judgment. It is not a show place, a beauty spot, but a revelation . . . it is the world's supreme example of erosion. But this is not what it really is. It is, I repeat, a revelation. The Colorado River made it, but you feel when you are there that God gave the Colorado River its instructions. It is all Beethoven's nine symphonies in stone and magic light. Even to remember that it is still there lifts up the heart. If I were an American, I should make my remembrance of it the final test of men, art, and policies. I should ask myself: Is this good enough to exist in the same country as the Canyon? How would I feel about this man, this kind of art, these political measures, if I were near that Rim? Every member or officer of the Federal Government ought to remind himself, with triumphant pride, that he is on the staff of the Grand Canyon."[1]

"The Grand Canyon is enough in itself to clear a whole continent from the charge of being dull." — J. B. Priestley. Helen agrees.

Elsewhere, Priestley declares "the Grand Canyon is enough in itself to clear a whole continent from the charge of being dull."

Some of the shortest Grand Canyon descriptions have been the most picturesque. Consider these:

"It is a land of music," was Major John Wesley Powell's journal entry.

"The divine abyss," John Burroughs called it, and . . ."the very womb of the world . . ." was the way Irvin S. Cobb described it.

"These are the footprints of Creation," said John C. Van Dyke. At another time he wrote, "It is not the eighth wonder of the world but the first."

Owen Wister pictured the Canyon "terrible as the Day of Judgment, sublime as the Psalms of David."[2]

And McCutcheon, once more, "you . . . get more sightseeing in one glance than is possible any place else in the world . . ."[3]

A former park superintendent tells of a child — a young girl — who, upon getting her first view of the Canyon, exclaimed, "What happened?"

Charles F. Lummis came at his observations of the Canyon obliquely: "I have seen people rave over it; better people struck dumb with it; even strong men who cried over it; but I have never yet seen the man or woman that expected it."[4]

Some of the Hopi Indians, however, perhaps did expect it, at least in the afterlife. According to William Hamilton Nelson, "Hopi Indians say Grand Canyon is an entrance to Heaven, and all we can say is that they have a wonderful sense of location."

Those who have put their minds and their pens to Grand Canyon portrayals have come up with nearly every approach that literature, science, psychology, or religion could afford.

One writer speculated on the effect the Canyon could exert on political leaders and concluded, "Hitler would have been a vastly different man, too, if he had only seen the Canyon . . . It debunks the ego like nothing else."[5]

We have quoted Irvin S. Cobb. This humorist of the early years of this century visited the Grand Canyon even before Francis and his brother went there. His descriptions, and often tongue-in-cheek observations, in his book ROUGHING IT,

"Terrible as the Day of Judgment, sublime as the Psalms of David." — Owen Wister.

DELUXE, were classics:

"Imagine . . . imagine . . . imagine . . . and if you imagine hard enough and keep it up long enough you may begin, in the course of eight or ten years, to have a faint, a very faint and shadowy conception of this spot . . ."[6]

"You are at the absolute jumping-off place. There is nothing between you and the undertaker except six thousand feet, more or less, of dazzling Arizona climate."[7]

"If ever Jehovah chose an earthly abiding place, surely this place of awful, unutterable majesty would be it."[8]

Edwin Corle wrote an entire book, LISTEN, BRIGHT ANGEL, dealing with varied aspects of the Canyon. Anthologist — and later the governor of Arizona, Bruce Babbitt — insisted that Corle "resisted the impulse to paint any visual images at all"[9] of this Arizona treasure. If he did not paint images, then he marshalled graphic phrases to depict people's reactions to the Canyon, or to give helpful advice concerning it. Sprinkled through the leaves of Corle's book, like refreshing dew on the tree leaves in a forest, are such glistening jewel drops as these:

". . . the music of Beethoven and Varese is to be heard; the painting of El Greco and Klee is to be seen; and the art of the Grand Canyon is to be experienced."[10]

"The reactions of people to the Grand Canyon are interesting. Most of them are honest. They just give up."[11]

". . . it unbalances most people's values . . ."[12]

". . . the Grand Canyon will give you a lot of clues as to the meaning of meaning. It can be just a hole in the earth or it can be a religious experience."[13]

In the final chapter of his book about Grand Canyon, Corle, who had perhaps resisted the temptation to describe it in his own words, declares, "In a Wordsworthian sense it has 'thoughts that do often lie too deep for tears.'"[14]

Through the years we, ourselves, have written whole pages and chapters of descriptive phrases trying to convey the Canyon's ultimate essence. In a certain sense, we could convey the two most profound characteristics which impress every serious and thoughtful visitor who ponders this enigmatic colossus, with what is probably the shortest description ever given:

? — !

Wonder — and awe. These two symbols seem to express it all.

"When we get to the Grand Canyon you children are not to touch a thing."

Interlude

THE FAMILY CIRCUS
Visits Grand Canyon

Writers with words, artists with paint, photographers with film — they all attempt to portray Grand Canyon. But there are also the cartoonists. With pen in hand and tongue in cheek, they *draw* it. Arizona cartoonist Bil Keane, read daily by more than 100 million Americans, is such a one. As a restful interlude, let's enjoy his imaginative creations as he takes THE FAMILY CIRCUS® on a Grand Canyon vacation.

[These 14 cartoons are used with the kind permission of The Register and Tribune Syndicate, Inc. by whom they are copyrighted.

They will tickle your funnybone.]

223

"I'd feel better if we had four leashes."

"Wish they had something like this between our
house and the school."

224

THE FAMILY CIRCUS   by Bil Keane

"It'd be easier if they had escalators."

'THE FAMILY CIRCUS   by Bil Keane .

"The ranger said the river dug the canyon,
Mommy, and you said God
did it. Who's right?"

225

"Why not?"

"Is this bus and the mules the only rides to go
on at the Grand Canyon?"

"After we see the sunrise, THEN can we all go back to bed?"

"This is like a church, Mommy. Everyone's whispering."

"Stop eating 'tato chips, Jeffy. We're tryin' to hear the river."

"Reminds me of that rainbow layer cake you made for my birthday."

THE FAMILY CIRCUS.   by Bil Keane

"Daddy's pictures will be better than these
'cause we'll be in them."

THE FAMILY CIRCUS,   by Bil Keane

"Why does Mommy hafta be alone to
medicate?"

THE FAMILY CIRCUS,   **by Bil Keane**

"That's gonna be a hard act to follow."

XXXIII

Dispelling a Myth, on Our 55th

1983

"Your 55th wedding anniversary? You shouldn't attempt hiking down that Canyon. You'll fall and break some bones. Especially if you go down the Kaibab Trail. It's too steep."

That, in essence, was the nature of the comments which we heard from several persons — including a physician — when it was learned that we would be hiking in and out of Grand Canyon on our 55th wedding anniversary, just as we had been doing since our 49th.

"Age has relatively little to do with it," might have been our answer. "The ability to hike the Canyon trails depends on keeping fit, exercising and eating properly, and maintaining an affirmative mental attitude."

Helen, in her so-called "middle age," experienced three separate falls — in and around our home — and broke a bone — in her wrist or foot — each time. Then she learned how to strengthen her bones through proper diet and calcium supplements. Now, at double the age of her bone-breaking experiences, she has less likelihood of a fracture or break than she did before she learned better.

She was once plagued with arthritis. Now — again through controlled, careful diet and regular exercise — that has been brought largely under control.

Francis, in his middle years, was overweight. Again, sensible diet and exercise. He shed one quarter of his avoirdupois.

We eliminated red meat. We drastically reduced intake of sweets. We cut out excess eating of every kind. Now we gorge on fruits. Helen loves gardening. So she planted a garden. She composts it with our kitchen scraps. Since we do most of our living on the second floor of our home, that means going downstairs, then digging in the compost pile. The result — more vigorous health for Helen, and fine vegetables for us both.

Those stairs are one of our heaven-sent "built-in" exercizers. We descend and ascend them an average of 20 times daily. When we hike from the Grand Canyon Rim to the river once a year, we descend approximately one mile in vertical elevation, and ascend that much coming out. In one year, going up and down the stairs of our house, the annual figure is 12 miles down and 12 miles up, in vertical elevation loss or gain. Stairways are footsteps to health.

We walk up and down steep hills three times weekly. We jog a bit. Through reading — and practice — we have learned the value of correct mental attitudes; of affirmative living. We don't neglect our spiritual life.

With all of these things going for us, why shouldn't we, as a 55th wedding anniversary celebration, hike down the steep South Kaibab Trail, to the river and Phantom Ranch?

Leaving trailhead on a May 1st day beset with clouds, we headed down. A small pool of frozen water winked at us in farewell.

Down! The South Kaibab Trail is sheer descent. Yesterday's mule tracks, frozen solid, made good stepholds for our cleated shoes, but frozen mud puddles were hard on our feet. A few small patches of snow, just below the Rim, gave us cool greetings. Far over on the North Rim we could make out large banks of the white stuff.

A series of steep switchbacks.

About a mile down, sheer dropoffs extending for several

Francis and Helen found that this Indian girl loves the Canyon as much as they do.

hundred feet on both sides of the trail. These made us stop to reminisce. Twenty years before we had made our only ascent by this route — at night.

Helen looked down over each edge, "I think I remember this place. I was scared."

The trail had widened to six or eight feet; there was no real danger, at least by daylight.

A sign: "Rim, 1½ miles. You have descended 1500 feet." This was Cedar Ridge. We stopped to rest, and to reminisce again. Around us was a gently sloping area, perhaps five acres in extent, of red hermit shale. Witchlike, bare juniper tree skeletons made dramatic statues against the sky. The live junipers were gnarled, bent by action of wind and weather. One end of the large area was graced with a public toilet. *Very* public. Its top, one side, and a strip around the bottom, were open. In the other direction, we visited a glassed-in display of fossils.

Time to move on.

Long switchbacks took us down from Cedar Ridge. A mule train approached. With no place to stand on the outside of the trail (it dropped off sheer), we squeezed into a crevasse on the inner side. Passing areas were scarce along here; this was as good as any. Ahead of us we could see a baker's dozen of switchbacks snaking downward. We snaked down with them. Then almost level for a ways. Then *real* switchbacks. Steep.

We stopped. But not because of the steepness. Over ahead, against the dark backdrop of Vishnu Temple, lightning streaked the sky. We listened. After a moment, thunder tumbled and echoed through the Canyon. This was a show! With sound effects.

Five minutes later came the show's second act. Rain. As fast as we could we rummaged in our packs for waterproof windbreakers. Black thunderheads encircled the temple formations to the east. White cumulus formations billowed over the North Rim. Thunder rumbled. Nature was murmuring her secrets to us.

The Tonto Platform is only a narrow strip at the point we crossed it, near the Tipoff. We scarcely were conscious of it on this 55th anniversary hike of ours. Probably because our thoughts were on the rain. But last year! We had made this same descent

The public toilet at Cedar Ridge is very *public.*

235

on our 54th and the Tonto Platform had been a flower garden then. No need to list the varieties. Just get ahold of any Flower Guide for this area and nearly every flower in the book had been blooming — last year — in celebration of that anniversary.

It was as though a rainbow had dropped from the sky. There were yellows, purples, whites, reds, blues. Mallows were strewn in the rocks. Daisies peeped from behind the mallows. Indian paintbrush painted the bare spots.

A dozen varieties of these flowers — hundreds of delicate blooms — were shaped like perfect stars.

Francis had jotted in his notebook: "I must look up at the sky tonight to see if Orion and the Pleiades are still there. Otherwise I think they may have tumbled earthward during the darktime hours and scattered in starry grandeur along this section of the Trail."

Less than half an hour later the rain was gone. Lunchtime and the most majestic view of the entire day arrived hand in hand. Trailmix, dried fruit from our packs, and water from a flask, were refreshing. But we really didn't need food or drink at this moment; we had one of the Canyon's best views to feast on, and a panorama of splendor to drink in, as we ate.

Just below us was the Colorado River, the principal sculptor of all this tumbled immensity. Last year its waters had been silver. Now they had turned to gold. At least deep chocolate yellow. The river was galloping through this mighty chasm laden with so much sediment — picked up from the late winter runoffs — that we could hear it groan under the weight. Before Glen Canyon Dam was built, up near the Utah border, the Colorado hauled off a million pick-up truckfuls, *every ordinary day.* Even now, with these heavy runoffs, it was carrying away vast quantities of soil. This gorge was being cut and scoured a trifle deeper — even though infinitesimally — right as we looked.

That gorge! This was very close to the spot where Francis and his brother, exactly 60 years and one month before, had stopped to absorb its multicolored granite-walled wonders. By roughest calculation, over 20 billion truck loads had been hauled off since then. Francis couldn't notice the difference. But we drank in the immensity, as nature's orchestra tuned up to provide background music. Song of birds. Gutteral rumbling roar of the

Colorado. Even Bright Angel Creek, joining the Colorado just below us, was adding its ruffle of drums to the orchestration, as it galloped and snorted downward with a speed and power that was moving boulders. The great rock amphitheater below us — this two billion-year-old colosseum of Vishnu schist — was vibrating with muted sounds. Muted thunder of water below. Then — repeat performance! muttering thunder overhead. Our peaceful lunch scene was rudely drenched with more rain.

We started down, over the most wicked part of the trail. First along and over red rock. Then the real switchbacks took command. Helen's feet began to throb. She changed to a pair of easier shoes, from our packs. It was hard for her to make the high steps over great logs, imbedded in the trail to stop runoff.

Wind! In addition to windbreakers, we had gotten out our ponchos. They flapped crazily in the gusts sweeping up from below. We were becoming soaked.

Just two more switchbacks and we could take shelter in the trail's only tunnel — leading to the suspension bridge across the river. Then:

HAIL!

We've been pummeled by hailstones in many parts of the world. But none like these. They were not unusually large. But they struck us with unusual force. They stung like bullets. Later we reasoned it out. All other hailstones which have ever fallen our way have come from storm clouds hanging low in the sky. Had we stood on the Rim to receive this beating of hail, that would have been the case in this storm.

But the Grand Canyon is different — in its hailstorms as in so many other respects. We were one vertical mile below the Rim. The hailstones fell from the clouds, found there was no earth beneath them where it should have been, so had to continue falling. With each foot of descent those stones gained speed. A mile down they were bulleting through empty space like a thousand tiny cannon balls. A hailstorm in the Canyon's depths, taking advantage of an extra mile of gravitational pull, produces effects like few other places on earth. It can be injurious to one's health. No wonder we ran for that tunnel.

It was crowded with hikers — lucky ones, who had gotten to that shelter before the rains and the hail. But after we had

Heading down! Bright Angel Creek and campground are at the right. The hikers' bridge leads across to the River Trail, at left.

The Kaibab Trail, leading down to the suspension bridge, passes through a tunnel. Tiny black dot at lower right is tunnel entrance.

joined them, we had momentary doubts. Not about them, but about what they were enduring. *This was a wind tunnel*, at least on this particular day. Gusts and blasts of air fury were whipping through it like a Texas Norther. The storm god's exhalations.

We groped our way farther back — into complete darkness. A bend in the tunnel cut out all light. When we reached the far end, the hail had ceased. But not the tempest. We stepped out onto the 440-foot-long suspension bridge leading across the great river. It was buffered on either side by heavy steel fencing. Otherwise we might have — at least so it seemed at the time — gone with the wind, right into the Colorado. About half a mile later, we were at Phantom Ranch.

Ice. Snow. Frozen mud. Lightning. Thunder. Hail. Wind. Accompanied by grandeur, all the way, the Grand Canyon had lived up to its name. It had pulled out all the stops for an anniversary celebration.

Near the conclusion of the meal that night, in the 50 seat dining hall — with every seat occupied by a hiker (the mule parties ate separately) — the Phantom Ranch manager made an announcement:

"We have a couple with us tonight who should be an inspiration to us all. Helen and Francis Line hike down here every year on their anniversary. Today is their 55th."

The applause drowned out all sounds of Bright Angel Creek, just outside. "Try to top that," someone shouted. A man from the next table gave Helen a huge kiss, and shook Francis' hand. Two others followed suit. A hiker from Switzerland shouted from across the room, "Which was harder, hiking down, or the 55 years?" When we got up to leave, they all applauded again.

One young man wearing a "Michigan" sweatshirt ran out of the building and stopped us. "My wife didn't dare ask you this, but she insisted that I do it. What is your secret for staying married so long?"

"It's because we're in love," spoke up Helen.

"Love — and complete unselfishness," Francis added.

At breakfast next day we were the king and queen of the party. The fellow hikers at our table vied with each other to serve us. Someone asked, "Are you stiff?"

"When I tried to get up, about 1 o'clock to go to the bathroom, I didn't think I could walk." That from Helen. Then she added, "But now I'm feeling just fine."

That is perhaps the test of good health — the ability of one's body to recoup after a good night's sleep.

When we departed Phantom Ranch we chose the longer Bright Angel route for our exit. The Kaibab Trail, on our descent, had already bestowed on us more than we had a right to ask. It had given us a storm-wrapped package of glowing memories for our 55th anniversary celebration.

XXXIV

Jottings at Phantom Ranch

Phantom Ranch cabins have perhaps the earliest check out time of any place in America — 8 a.m. In many hotels and motels the guests aren't even up by then.

*   *   *

On our 50th anniversary visit to Phantom, hikers and the mule parties ate dinner and breakfasts together — with nearly inch-thick steaks for all. Then the perennial problem of crowding — too many customers — changed the system. Now, the mule folks dine at 6 p.m. — with steaks. Hikers eat at 7 — with beef stew. In our opinion, the stew beats the steaks. It is laden with vegetables. The later hour also allows more time for resting and writing — after that strenuous descent.

Breakfast for mule parties is now at 7 a.m. Hikers eat at 6, and can get the much-needed early start to help avoid afternoon heat. But if you are staying over a day or so, you eat breakfast at 6 or 7, regardless. No sleeping in, at Phantom.

*   *   *

243

On our earlier Phantom visits the cook knocked on our doors to waken us. Now each cabin is equipped with an alarm clock. Automation has even reached the Canyon depths. But whether cook-knock or alarm, woe be to those who are late. No breakfast!

*　*　*

In the Phantom Ranch staff dining room hangs this sign:
> Please do not
> annoy, torment,
> pester, plague,
> molest, worry,
> badger, harry,
> harass, heckle,
> persecute, irk,
> bully, vex,
> disquiet, grate,
> beset, bother,
> tease, nettle,
> tantalize, or
> ruffle the animals

*　*　*

Next to us, as we ate our evening stew, with all the trimmings, was a couple from the Netherlands, down here to explore Grand Canyon. In her soft voice the woman said, "We don't have anything like this in Holland."

Understatement of the year!

"But you have the world's finest tulips."

"Yes, we'll be back home next week — in time to see them bloom."

*　*　*

Meals were enlivened with what the manager called his "Grand Canyon Information Hour." Example: "Here at the Ranch, you may have noticed all the irrigation ditches — to flood the trees. Those ditches are dry now. You should be careful walking around after dark. Some of our help have taken first aid courses. But they may not be too good at fixing a broken leg.''

*　　*　　*

Americans poke fun at the postman who goes for a walk on his holiday. That is no joke here. Most of the young rangers, as well as many of the workers at Phantom Ranch, Bright Angel, and in Grand Canyon Village spend their free days hiking up or down the Canyon trails or to its more remote areas. One reason they work here is because they love it so much. Their most satisfying vacation is to go exploring. Each hike, even over familiar trails, is a new discovery; the Canyon takes on a new face with every change of hour or season. The Phantom workers have ten days on, and four off. Four-day ''weekends'' allow for a lot of exploring.

*　　*　　*

Major John Wesley Powell named Bright Angel Creek. He put ashore here on August 15, 1869, on his boat journey of discovery down the Colorado. If he'd come along here right now, he'd have definitely called it something else. This torrent isn't *Bright,* in the sense of clarity, on this May morning; its racing waters are thick with sediment dislodged all the way along its mad course down from the North Rim. It is not a *Creek,* but a wildly charging river. And certainly no *Angel* ever looked or acted like this. Had Powell happened by at a time such as this (and they are rather rare, we understand) he would have had to call it something else. Actually, he named this stream Bright Angel, in contrast to a turbulent muddy tributary they had encountered much earlier and which they had dubbed ''Dirty Devil.''

*　　*　　*

Bright Angel Creek, this year, is on a spree — the wildest we've ever seen it. Boulders are clashing against each other as

245

Bright Angel Creek is swollen from the melting snow.

they are being tumbled downstream. The frantic brown waters are racing like an untamed child plunging into adolescense to see what lies ahead.

Plenty! First, the great Colorado itself — its swirls and depths and roars and rapids. Then the dizzying plunge over the Hoover Dam spillways, and encounters with half a dozen other dams beyond. After that, the Sea of Cortez, with a battering inflow and outflow of tides which are among the highest and strongest in the West. Finally, little Bright Angel will be swallowed up and lost, in the vast Pacific. If she only knew what lay ahead, perhaps she'd slow down and linger here awhile. Few spots in her future can be better than this.

*   *   *

With all the gear we packed down here to Phantom Ranch, we forgot one thing — which we'll surely bring next trip. It seemed so unnecessary here that we never even thought of it. In all this punch bowl of vastness, one would think that the most likely aid to vision would be a telescope or field glasses. They would help, for there is more here in way of distances than the unaided eye can take in.

But the thing we forgot is a microscope.

For this Canyon is not only vast — it is intricate. Its depths are not only to be measured in miles, but in millimeters. It is made up, not only of sky-scraping monoliths — but of tiny flecks of mica, particles of billion-year-old rock, and even powdered red dust. It displays miniature flowers, perfectly shaped, though as small as the head of a pin. For those with time to tarry, the Canyon's gifts of Lilliputian creations are endless; delicate lichens, patterned algae, diminutive roots, minikin shoots, miniature stems. Even tiny ants and insects. They are all a part of Grand Canyon. We need a microscope. Small is beautiful, too.

*   *   *

One idle day at Phantom, we walked back to pay homage to the suspension bridge across the Colorado. On the downward hike one is just too preoccupied to survey it properly.

247

Bright Angel Creek galloping to join the Colorado.

There are two bridges, of course. The more recent one — a smaller affair — is for the Bright Angel Trail hikers. It was constructed, primarily, to support the large pipe through which water is conveyed to South Rim. Originating at Roaring Springs, far above Phantom Ranch, water flows by gravity this far. Then the buildup of sheer pressure pushes it on *up* hill to Indian Gardens, from where it is pumped to the top. This bridge is not used by the mules, which seem to be frightened at its open-grilled flooring. They continue a short distance to the Kaibab Trail bridge — the one we had headed out to inspect. When we had reached the Kaibab bridge, we surveyed it for a moment in wonder.

"Wouldn't you like to have been here when it was being built? It would have been a sight!"

It certainly would. The 440-foot-long steel structure is supported by two enormous cables, each 550 feet long, each weighing 2320 pounds. How to get them down from the Rim? Mules? No way. Helicopters? Out of the question. Forty-two Havasupai Indians, strung out along the tenth-of-a-mile length of each cable, hoisted it on their shoulders, then skillfully made their way down all those rugged descents and zigzags, like some strange giant centipede from another world.

Helen suggested that the sight of that 84-legged writhing black snake could very well have given rise to a New World myth — "The Grand Canyon Monster."

She observed also that in the building of the West, many of its "impossible" feats had been accomplished by the American Indians, such as here, by the Chinese who did much of California's hardest early day railroad construction, and Mexicans who labored at difficult tasks everywhere. We extend our heartfelt "Thanks" to them all. Especially to those 42 native Americans who became the "legs" for those giant cables.

*   *   *

Our children and grandchildren were brought up on Kenneth Graham's WIND IN THE WILLOWS. In one of its favorite passages, could that author have been thinking about this Phantom Ranch haven, where Bright Angel meets the Colorado? Here

249

Helen and the suspension bridge are surrounded by the two billion-year-old rocks of the granite gorge.

is the passage:

"And you really live by the river? What a jolly life! 'By it and with it and on it and in it' said the Rat. It's brother and sister to me, and aunts, and company, and food and drink, and (naturally) washing. It's my world, and I don't want any other. What it hasn't got is not worth having, and what it doesn't know is not worth knowing. Lord, the times we've had together!''

We applaud those sentiments. What times *we* have had in the Grand Canyon, which a river helped create!

XXXV

Hiking the Inner Trails

"Despite the problems, despite the intimate hazards, and even though the demands on human energy are enormous, going by foot is still the best way to travel the trails of the Grand Canyon. You can go at your own pace, stop when you wish, linger at will, hurry or loaf, and be completely at ease.!"[1]

That is the assessment of ranger-naturalists Ann and Myron Sutton, in their excellent book, THE WILDERNESS WORLD OF THE GRAND CANYON.

But they also sprinkle the pages of their book with observations which serve as warnings.

"Park rangers can talk by the hour of rescue operations to bring out the dead and injured."[2]

". . . the major causes of human fatalities in the park are heart attacks — exertion at 7,000 feet can be dangerous to the unaware — and accidents resulting from reckless driving."[3]

"The margin for error in this Canyon is not very wide," the Suttons stress, and characterize it as having ". . . some of the

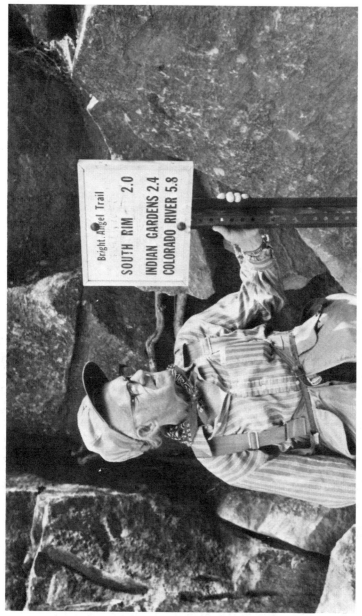

Bright Angel Trail

SOUTH RIM 2.0
INDIAN GARDENS 2.4
COLORADO RIVER 5.8

It's a hot day, and still several miles to go.

254

It's a cold day, but the Lines make it out of the Canyon without slipping.

most severe hiking environments in North America."[4]

They go on:

"Inner-canyon trails have taken the lives of many hikers. If there was ever a place where men can test the limits of their endurance and self-reliance, it is within this Canyon. Heat, thirst, hunger, danger, isolation, and disaster become the unwanted partners of the unprepared. But they are also part of the adventure, and if properly prepared, hikers may enjoy some unparalleled experiences within this Canyon."[5]

W. E. Garrett, Associate Editor of National Geographic Magazine, writing in the July, 1978 issue, says, ". . . as many as 12 hikers a day with more enthusiasm than endurance and good sense collapse and have to be 'dragged out' of the canyon.:[6]

Then Garrett makes the amazing statement:

"Under summer sun the surface temperature may reach 200°F."[7]

The Geographic is a highly regarded magazine. We have written and photographed for it, and respect it.

But we questioned that statement. In the Canyon's depths it has sometimes *seemed* to us that the temperature was close to the 212°F boiling point, but we really didn't think it actually ever reached 200°.

Back in California we queried the director-naturalist of the Living Desert Reserve, near Palm Springs, asking what a 120° thermometer reading in the shade (which we have observed in Grand Canyon) might be at surface level in the sun. Along came this reply, from Director-Naturalist Karen Sausman.

"In answer to your question, when the air temperature reaches 120° it is quite possible for the ground surface temperature in the sun to reach 180°. When we hear a weather report on the radio it gives the air temperature 5 feet above the ground in the shade. Obviously, when you are out on the desert hiking there is no simple way to levitate yourself 5 feet above the ground in a shady area!"

Her answer was based on open desert conditions. At the bottom of the rock-enclosed Canyon gorge, with surface rocks reflecting heat into one's face like a mirror, perhaps 200° was a correct figure. No wonder we perspired!

And no wonder that, on hike after hike in Grand Canyon,

we have had to render aid and assistance, and often share our water, food, and rain gear, with those who went ill-prepared or failed to shepherd their strength and their supplies. Most often, we found that those requiring aid were young men, who looked physically strong and sturdy.

One such young man, years ago, had a frightening experience which, had it ended tragically, would have changed world history. Twenty-nine year old John J. Pershing became lost in the Canyon, along with three of his friends. They nearly perished of thirst before being rescued by a Havasupai Indian. When Pershing commanded the American Expeditionary Forces in World War I, he is reported to have wished that the Grand Canyon could have been moved to Europe, to form a barrier between Germany and France.

A caution notice issued by Park Superintendent Merle Stitt, when he was serving at the park, contained a subtle hint that adequate precautions should be taken.

WARNING: THE SUPERINTENDENT OF GRAND
CANYON NATIONAL PARK HAS DETERMINED
THAT HIKING IN MANY PARTS OF THE CANYON
CAN BE DANGEROUS TO YOUR HEALTH

Besides heat, high altitude, and isolation, there is another enemy. The ranger-naturalists, the Suttons, say:

"We have also repeatedly seen people who dared not get within twenty feet of the rim, people petrified with an acrophobic fear that they might, uncontrollably, jump in. They actually feared the Canyon, as if it stirred in them some wholly inhuman dementia."[8]

For those who penetrate *below* the Rim, mule riders exhibit more fear than do hikers. Several times we have encountered riders who tell us they have kept their eyes closed almost the entire way down, too fearful to look at the abysses below. Why they assay the trip at all, we cannot understand.

Irvin Cobb describes the first moments of the Canyon mule-ride in his droll fashion:

"The thought comes to you that, after all, it is a very bright and beautiful world you are leaving behind. You turn your head to give it a long, lingering farewell, and try to put your mind on something cheerful — such as your life insurance."[9]

257

"The Canyon can be dangerous to your health." Luckily the authors
happened along after these rocks had fallen.

Cobb's description of Bright Angel Trail is excellent:

"Imagine a trail that winds like a snake and climbs like a goat and soars like a bird, and finally bores like a worm and is gone . . ."[10]

Two choice spots on the South Rim afford superb views of portions of the trail. Perhaps those planning for the first time to hike down Bright Angel, or later to come back up, should not seek out these particular Rim views until their inner Canyon experience is over. What one sees is almost too revealing — too discouraging.

One of these view spots is at Grandeur Point, on the short Rim trail, north of the visitor center, and west of Yavapai Museum. The most severe switchbacks are not visible — concealed by great shoulders of rock — but enough of the snakelike serpentine trail does show — all in one instantaneous vertical view — to quicken one's heart beat just standing there, looking.

The other prime viewpoint is from Trail View I, on West Rim Drive, about half a mile from Bright Angel Lodge. Several times we have taken our 42 power telescope to that point, set it up on a tripod, and spent an afternoon studying the hikers as they climbed the last three miles out to South Rim. This telescope is powerful enough to bring out the rings of Saturn or the moons of Jupiter. Focused on the struggling — and often staggering — hikers, it reveals nearly every aspect of their agonies as they inch upward toward the top. No wonder, when hiking up ourselves, we have had to offer aid in so many instances. People go down Grand Canyon who have no conception of the difficulties required to climb back out!

XXXVI

Return to North Rim

1983

Three almost completely different meanings are wrapped up in the first word of the Grand Canyon's title. "Grand," according to Webster, means:

1. Marked by great magnificence. Fine or imposing in appearance.

2. Having higher rank or more dignity than others having the same general designation.

3. Of large size, extent. Of a size conferring distinction.

The qualities inherent in the first two of these definitions wove such a spell over us that with every Canyon visit we often became intoxicated — almost drunk — with the magnificence. Absorbing the beauty taxed us physically. We had come to expect that problem. But the third meaning — the Canyon's sheer size and extent — presented another dilemma.

We began to find that Grand Canyon is so enormous that, even for those who love it, portions of it may be neglected for extended periods of time. We had become so caught up in the lure of the South Rim's trails and viewpoints — combined with our new love, Supai and the magic waterfalls — that the North Rim went, for a long period, completely unattended by us. There were other contributing circumstances. The North Rim season is short. And on our May 1 wedding anniversary — the one day of the year that we *always* head Canyonward — the North Rim and Kaibab Forest are clothed in impassable snows.

Absence perhaps does make the heart grow fonder. When we returned to this area which we had neglected, just at the moment that late summer was flirting with early autumn, in 1983, each vista seemed like a new world which we had never discovered before.

Jacob Hamblin — at least a large oil portrait of him hanging in the Jacob Lake Lodge — welcomed us to this Kaibab-North Rim world of grandeur and isolation.

The isolation is complete, more so than nearly any other large area in the United States. Visitors come, of course, by driving a couple of hundred miles from the South Rim. But no newspapers are available for purchase, no magazines. The Jacob Lake Inn can get TV reception — a couple of stations boosted in from Salt Lake. But the Kaibab Lodge and the North Rim Lodge are mercifully removed from television influence, although they are trying to draw in a signal from Bill Williams Mountain west of Flagstaff. The North Rim rangers can see their voting precinct, ten miles away, on South Rim, but they need to drive the 200 miles, or commandeer a helicopter, to cast their votes.

When the geography of an area bars the daily news — and even the voting activities associated with the political process — it can be considered isolated. A unique experience for the 1980s.

The ghost of Jacob Hamblin rode with us as we left the tiny spot which bears his first name and headed upward and southward into the Kaibab Forest. The ''lake'' itself is a mile to the west — a nearly dried-up pond of brownish water no larger than a few saddle blankets spread out on the ground to dry. That lake, however, and others like it scattered over the Kaibab Plateau, mean the difference between life and death for the forest animals which inhabit this land. These geological sink holes filled with melting snows are their source of drinking water.

Jacob Hamblin himself probably meant the difference between life and death for many of the early explorers — and the Indians — of the whole Grand Canyon region. During the middle years of the nineteenth century this Mormon pioneer was something like a "Johnnie Appleseed" of mercy, scattering seeds of friendship, help, and goodwill wherever he went, appearing first here then there, all the way from Lee's Ferry to the land of the Havasupai. He was the friend of every Indian tribe in this part of the West; he befriended them, and they trusted him as one of their own. The place which bears the first half of his name — either the "lake" or the wide place in the road — is so small that most people miss it altogether, but Jacob Hamblin was a man who deserves a large and enduring monument. His spirit rode with us as we penetrated the Kaibab Forest.

The road gradually ascended through a world of pines and aspens, transporting us deeper and deeper into the land of isolation. Then the forest parted, to make a lush Kaibab meadow.

A mile or so down the road there was another meadow. And then another. And another. And another.

Some of them were small, some large, opening up grass-clothed parks in the deep forest which were like — well, there is no other word for it; these meadows turned this vast jungle of trees into a series of natural, sylvan *parks*. Parks undisturbed by humans; unscarred by civilization. We recalled a wall motto we'd read back at the Jacob Lake Inn:

"The Lord created the Kaibab Forest on the sixth day so he could rest there on the seventh."

This was the Sabbath, we suddenly realized, as we were penetrating this wonderland of the Kaibab. This was the "seventh day" and the creator of these meadows was resting. The whole world was resting. The isolation, the quiet, the ageless beauty and wonder of this North Rim world was seeping once again into our veins and making new persons of us. We had returned!

At one of the meadows the isolation was temporarily broken. Tucked back on the far side of a great expanse of openness in the forest was Kaibab Lodge and we were soon absorbing the warmth from its great fireplace as we visited with Cliff Cox, son of the couple who had established this tiny oasis in the Kaibab years before. He filled us in on the details of three scenic areas which, providentially, we had never before visited. It is always good to have new fields to explore. By side roads east from Kaibab Lodge, three Grand Canyon viewpoints can easily be reached — East Rim, Marble Canyon, and Saddle Mountain.

"Marble Canyon View is best" said a girl at the lodge, so we decided to do that first.

What the comparative quality of the scenes would be, we would not know until our explorations were over, but the roads leading into them were, in themselves, enough to make the explorations worthwhile. Ten thousand young aspens had sprung up in the soil which had been stirred and broken as the narrow road had been put through. A breeze caressed their branches, and a million leaves lining our way began shaking and shimmering like the clicking tambourines of Spanish dancers. The whole forest was shivering deliciously.

These dancing leaves were green but then, rounding a bend in the narrow road, we plunged into a world of gold. The aspens had changed color. Autumn had won out over summer. A million clicking *golden* tambourines were stirring the world alive.

From our narrow road, a still narrower one branched off toward Marble Canyon View. Grass not only lined the sides, but lined the middle. Throughout our entire day we would encounter only one car. No newspapers. No television. Almost no cars. A woods trail in place of a freeway. Isolation!

But a magician must have been somewhere about. He waved his magic veil and we suddenly emerged from pines and aspens to behold a great cliff escarpment, then down and below, House Rock Valley, with the Vermillion Cliffs in the background. The gash of the Grand Canyon cut through the far edge of the scene.

This had been the favorite viewpoint of the girl at Kaibab Lodge. But, for us, Saddle Mountain viewpoint was better. Fourteen miles of an enchanted woods road, winding and dipping and climbing, led us to it. Much of the Marble Canyon View was visible from here, but also we looked out eastward toward another portion of Grand Canyon. Immediately below us was the deep cut of Saddle Canyon, looking as narrow as a knife blade. And just out beyond us, reached easily by hiking trail, beckoned Saddle Mountain itself. We climbed it. We lunched on ripe wild raspberries as we climbed, which was partial recompense for the destructive clawing of the berry bushes. Surrounding us were 12 giant dead skeletons of trees. We were in an isolated world of beauty.

East Rim View, though less dramatic, was good too, and the narrow forest road which led to it added to the touch of isolation.

* * * * * * *

Cape Royal, 20 miles east and south of the North Rim's Grand Canyon Lodge, is reached by paved highway. Tour buses include it on their schedules. A sense of apprehension traveled with us as we turned our car onto the road which would lead us back to this place where, in a series of half a dozen different visits, we had obtained the most significant motion pictures of our filming careers. That was at the time that World War II was ending, in 1945, when a hummingbird and a thistle plant had upstaged the giant Grand Canyon itself. (see Chapters 15 and 16)

The thistle, we discovered, was gone. Even if a hummingbird — perhaps a great-great grandchild of the one we filmed — had been in the vicinity, it would have been frightened away by a busload of German tourists who had timed their arrival to coincide with ours. For nearly an hour we waited, until all visitors were gone.

Cape Royal had changed. The vegetation, the trees, were different. Different paths to viewpoints had been constructed. There was an expansive parking area, and we could not even find where we had camped, in 1945.

We waited for the sunset hour. That, except for lack of hummingbird, was as dramatic as it had been nearly 40 years before. With yet another added attraction which we would soon discover — a phenomenon that perhaps no one else has witnessed from this cape.

Sunset was at 6:32 p.m. At 6 o'clock, shadows began to creep up the red formations about us. We were looking westward toward the sun. Five minutes before the sunset hour a gloom of approaching darkness began to swallow most of the Canyon, but Wotan's Throne still stood out.

A three-quarter moon shown in the sky above Desert View on the South Rim. With our field glasses we could easily see the Watch Tower over there. A wind suddenly whipped up out of the depths. The pine and juniper limbs shivered and swayed. A low moaning of restless branches filled the air.

The sun touched the distant westward horizon, with everything else down in the Canyon, in that direction, becoming grey and subdued. The golden ball itself was now easy to look at, without injury to the eyes. It takes approximately three minutes, after that first horizon contact, for the sun to disappear. We looked at our watches. The earth had swallowed up half of the orb. Now only a small segment of the disc was visible.

Something suddenly clicked in Francis' brain. Almost as though it were a repeat of the hummingbird episode of nearly 40 years before, he called out to Helen. "Quick, look for the green flash."

That requires an explanation:

From our view over the Pacific Ocean back at our home in California we had acquired the habit, just at the sunset hour, of looking for what is known as the "green flash." It is a phenomenon a bit hard to comprehend. At the moment the sun dips below the horizon, its white light is broken up into all the colors of the spectrum. The earth's atmosphere absorbs every color, up to green, the wave lengths of which are least affected by atmospheric absorption. At the instant of sunset, just as the disc disappears, there is sometimes — but not always — an instantaneous tiny green flash. One would not notice it unless he were trained to observe it. On rare occasions the last bit of the sun's disc itself will turn green just before disappearing. (We were careful, always, if the sun was bright or undimmed by mists, to view it through a piece of exposed film, or dark glass, to avoid eye injury).

Where the horizon is unobstructed and flat, this green flash phenomenon can be observed best. Ocean horizons are ideal.

But the western skyline at Cape Royal was unobstructed and flat. Had we not thought about the green flash possibility, we would have missed it altogether, for one must be intent on that, and nothing else. But, "Look for the green flash," Francis suddenly called.

We looked. We saw. We thrilled. There it was, instantaneous but definite and clear. In talking with rangers, Fred Harvey employees, and others, we have never run across anyone who has observed this phenomenon on either Rim. Perhaps —

just perhaps — this was another Grand Canyon "first."

The sky darkened; the Canyon depths gulped up nearly all remaining light. Then — as though miraculously revived by some hidden new life — the sky turned pink. The Canyon forms came back into light. The hue of the sky deepened to dark rose. The Canyon walls followed suit. Then darkness again.

We waited for another encore but that was the final curtain. The moon brightened in the sky. We saw a car light over on South Rim. As we took the winding road back to North Rim Lodge (no camping permitted now at Cape Royal) our car lights fell on the white aspens, turning them into tall slender ghosts scattered through the pine forest. Suddenly, four young deer appeared in the road right before us. We slowed nearly to a stop. Frightened, they eyed us timidly, then bounced away. We drove slowly for the rest of those 20 miles, taking no risk that we might strike a frightened deer. Also, we needed time to digest the miracles of our latest Cape Royal visit.

XXXVII

Grand Canyon Is a Weather Bowl

1983

Old-timers, wanting to prophesy Grand Canyon's weather, would survey the sky, or consult an almanac, or listen to the bay of coyotes. Now, a hiker preparing for his backpack journey into the Canyon, simply dials 638-2245. (From out of state one precedes those numbers with the Arizona area code, 602). A tape-recorded voice gives the weather forecast for the North and South Rims and for Phantom Ranch, current high and low temperatures, a summary of yesterday's weather, time of sunrise and sunset, road conditions, and other pertinent information a Canyon visitor might want.* Dial tones have replaced the songs of the coyotes.

This is understandable. Weather is important here. It has been a principal ingredient in the Canyon's formation and its geological history, as well as its ability to provide constantly changing spectacles for the unending flow of visitors. Because of weather, Grand Canyon is never the same, from one season to the next, one month to the next, one day to the next. It can be transformed, with complete change of costumes and makeup, as quickly as a stage actor who is filling multiple roles in a play.

269

Just at dusk one evening Francis saw what looked like the streaming white smoke of a forest fire pouring down into Bright Angel Fault. Going out to the Rim for a better view, he realized that it was fog. The Canyon, already nearly swallowed up by darkness, was filling with the white stuff as though this was an enormous stream of boiling water rushing in to fill a Paul Bunyan bathtub.

Francis followed the Rim walk up to the lighted area in front of Bright Angel Lodge. Fog filled the Canyon to within just a few feet of the Rim. The strong lights before the Lodge lit up the white contents.

As he looked out into the abyss, there on the white surface of the fog just below, he could see his shadow. He waved his hands and the huge black object down there echoed the motions. As he walked back and forth, his shadow strode back and forth also — a giant black figure stalking the Canyon depths, suspended and levitated — there in the mighty chasm.

Next day, the fog was gone. It was replaced by falling snow as the two of us spent much of the morning in the Yavapai Museum on the Rim. The exhibits there warrant hours of study but on this occasion our research was interrupted by a lady ranger.

"Our lecture was scheduled for outside," she announced, "but the weather is a bit bad. We'll try to carry on in here."

A large group of Japanese tourists came in just in time to join us. Crouching or sitting on the floor, some standing, we heard a heartwarming discussion of the geological wonders which lay just outside, below us.

"Are there any questions?"

A Japanese man spoke up, his words laced with strong accent. "When is best time to come to Canyon, so I can see? When is the weather good?"

The ranger accompanied her reply with an apologetic smile. "That is one question which I cannot answer with certainty. Yesterday was clear. Tomorrow may be. But winter snows and summer thunderstorms can come without any warning. The Grand Canyon weather is unpredictable."

We rose from our reclining postures and started to file out.

"Nice," murmured a Japanese woman who was obviously

270

the questioner's wife. "Nice — but *unpredictable.*"

Helen and I went outside, and came face to face with what that Japanese couple had probably seen but which we — who had been in the museum for considerable time — had missed. The snow had ceased, and the fog had returned with a vengeance.

The Grand Canyon, in full 11:30 o'clock-in-the-morning daylight, had been completely erased. It was gone, as though a magician had been at work. Stretching out from the Rim was an unending foam-like carpet of white. In Chicago, according to Carl Sandburg, the fog creeps in on cat's feet. This wasn't the way it had happened here. In the intervening hour since we had last looked out, the fog had leaped in like a Burmese tiger, to swallow the Canyon completely.

We've heard of tourists going to Alaska, spending as much as two weeks in McKinley National Park, and never seeing the mountain. But it had never occurred to us that anyone could come all the way from Japan to visit Grand Canyon, and then not see it.

These Japanese tourist parties sometimes make their visits brief. The average Grand Canyon visitor spends only two hours here, and only 20 minutes of that in viewing the Canyon itself. We held the hope that the Japanese couple and their friends, who had learned that the weather is "unpredictable," were able to stay until the fog lifted.

Grand Canyon weather is a forecaster's nightmare. It is not only unpredictable; it sometimes changes even as fresh bulletins are being issued.

At Grandview Point, on an autumn morning in 1983, we had a cloud display that, when we attempted to jot descriptions of it in our notebook, resulted in a mishmash of metaphors which would have dismayed a literary purist. We rate it as one of the best — and one of the most astonishing and beautiful — displays that the Grand Canyon has ever given us.

The morning was stormy. Driving along the Rim, and stopping at different viewpoints, we encountered only dull scenes of unlighted grayness, or misty indistinctness, or complete "white outs" of fog. What happened that morning made us realize that the Canyon not only changes from hour to hour, and minute to minute, but displays totally different aspects from mile to mile along its length.

As the authors hike the Canyon trails they find that the weather is a forecaster's nightmare.

We stopped at Grandview, expecting the same blah aspect that all the other viewpoints had offered — even those close by. We were stunned into action by the incredible sight which unfolded.

Helen snapped up a full role of film while Francis attempted to keep up with the display before us with jottings in our notebook. Our motion picture cameras might have done it partial justice; nothing else could, except on-the-spot eyewitness.

White foamy cloud masses were swirling around nearly every peak and temple in the wide area of our view. Cottony clusters of it suddenly burst up out of the depths to engulf great sections of the Canyon. Then there was just as sudden a reversal, and the scattered masses of white flowed back down, and disappeared, leaving the scene as it had been before. Then, as suddenly, it all surged up again.

Great fingers of the white dragon-like foam slithered out and encircled the temples, as though to devour them, and then disappeared.

At the same instant, one cloud of fog would be swirling in one direction while another white mass would rush by it, going the opposite way.

One moment, the view of the Colorado River in the gorge far below would be uncluttered and clear. Less than a minute later there would be no river at all. It was as though a great curtain had closed over the lower gorge.

Curls, swirls, floating ghosts. A ballet of white-robed dancers pirouetting through the abyss. Some giant with a mighty bellows, Helen speculated between camera shots, must be down below there somewhere. A three-ring aesthetic circus.

One *has* to mix metaphors; half a dozen differing impressions were storming into our consciousness simultaneously. We had proof that this display was a rarity. For nearly the entire time, Francis was broken out in gooseflesh, not from the cold — which was now intense — but from the glory of it all.

An ominous darkness began creeping in, but the yo-yo movements and gyrations of the clouds down below accelerated. It was as though the concealed puppeteer who was maneuvering and controlling all this action was breathless to get the entire act completed before the final curtain. Another change of metaphors, and it was over.

273

Back at the lodge, we were presently observing disgruntled tourists twiddling their digital watches in the lounge or moping in the bars, lamenting their ill fortune at having arrived at the Canyon on such a dismal day. They had missed one of the greatest shows on earth.

Grand Canyon is exciting — weather or no.

XXXVIII

Time Marches On

As we come over from California to Arizona toward the end of April each year, preparatory to our May 1 wedding anniversary hike into Grand Canyon, we experience the annual confusion of TIME. In April, the nation's clocks are turned ahead. Daylight Saving Time officially begins.

Everywhere, that is, except Arizona. This is a state of individualists--old-fashioned western, cowboy-type diehards. Why should they kowtow (no pun intended) to the national whim? Why should they be concerned with saving daylight? This clear-skied, open-horizoned state--so they reason--has daylight to spare. *Daylight Saving? Forget it.* So Arizona keeps on Mountain Standard the year round.

All of Arizona, that is, except the Indian reservations. These native Americans--and who can blame them?--are becoming as independent as the native Arizonans. Why should the red brothers (and sisters) stick to Mountain Standard Time just because the white brothers do? So every April the Indians turn their clocks ahead to Mountain Daylight Saving.

Some of the Indians, that is. The state of Arizona has nearly two dozen different, independent reservations, each more or less a nation unto itself. The Hopis are at odds, these days, in many ways, with the Navajos. Why should they go to Daylight Saving just because their Indian neighbors do? The Apaches to the south, the Pimas to the west, may have other independent ideas. The Yumans are close to their kin in California. Rather than switching to Mountain Daylight Saving Time on this last Sunday in April it may suit their whim to continue on Mountain Standard, which is the same as Pacific Daylight Time just across the Colorado River.

Then, on the first of May, we started (on Mountain Standard Time leaving the Rim) our annual hike down into the Canyon.

Here, the real shock came. The Grand Canyon is the one place in the world whose existence — whose very creation — is built and dependent on TIME. But man-made time? Perish the thought. In the Canyon one begins to understand what time is all about. That long hike from the South Rim, down Bright Angel Trail to the Colorado River and Phantom Ranch, is a journey, not through space, but through time.

The hiking distance is nothing. As the raven glides, it is only a few miles. But timewise — now you are talking. At least the rocks which surround you are talking. Here, instead of red man's and white man's time, the Canyon records its time by the color of its *rocks*.

The upper layer — the sedimentary deposits through which our hike started — wasn't even worth mentioning on nature's cosmic clock. It was only a couple of hundred million years old. But soon we descended to a point where the clock had really been ticking — to the great Redwall Formation. This 500-foot layer of limestone, tinted red by iron deposits from untold millennial drippings from the Supai layers above, has been 330 million years in the making — give or take a few millions. To grasp the breathtaking scope of all this, one needs to focus on that word "millennial." A millennium is a thousand years. In one million years there are one thousand millenniums. If our computer is correct (and this Grand Canyon is a locale that can drive the best of computers crazy), 330 million years represent three hundred and thirty thousand millenniums. It becomes apparent that one needs to expand the English language for use in this Canyon.

The next major layer we encounter is the Muav limestone,

500 million years old. But we've only commenced. To avoid brain fatigue (although every visitor to the Canyon depths gets it if he seriously ponders the age of his surroundings) — to avoid mental collapse, let's come to grips with the time-clock below the Devil's Corkscrew as we approach the Colorado River itself. We're marching downward through the layer of the Vishnu schist.

Speak that name with veneration. Hold it to your heart. Memorize it. Repeat it reverently. You are standing in the presence of the Eternal. You are walking (or riding muleback) through some of the older rocks on earth. The Grand Canyon is one of the few spots on earth where man (or woman, or child, for they come here too) can conveniently get down to a depth where ancient rocks such as this are visible. Here is what seems like the very beginning of TIME.

Two billion years is too much for us to grasp. It might help to explain that this area is thought to have once been as high as the Himalayas of India — from which the name Vishnu derives. Time, aided by the river and air and ice and all the elements, has worn it down to a present elevation of 2500 feet.

Standing here below the Corkscrew, looking at all the twists, and strains, and sprains and contortions of the exposed rock surface that represent the marks of two billion years, we began to realize that it didn't really matter whether our watches were on Mountain Standard Time, or Daylight Saving. The Grand Canyon goes on Geological Time. It throbs to a clock rhythm all its own. Its dial is Eternity itself.

The park service has endeavored to represent this graphically in an exhibit at the South Rim's Yavapai Museum. On an enormous "three minute" wall clock, each tick represents 11 million years. The Vishnu schist in the Canyon's floor was deposited at the first tick of the clock, two billion years ago. In the final second of this three minute program, the Colorado River began its work, and human beings appeared on earth.

One of humankind's latest gadgets, the digital quartz watch, might very well have been dreamed up right here in Grand Canyon. The time-keeping element in the new watches is a tiny sliver of quartz rock, which pulsates or vibrates at a constant rate of thousands of impulses per second. Did some pecuniary genius one day stand on the Rim of this Canyon and exclaim, "Egad, think of all the watches that could be made from the granite in that gorge below."

But did he also think: "If each tiny sliver of quartz is pulsating thousands of times per second, how many pulsations would that be in two billion years?" It would take the figure 1, followed by a complete book of zeros, even to approximate the figure.

If Grand Canyon is to be compared with any timepiece made by humans it would have to be called the great-great-great grandfather clock of the ages.

In one of the annual contests of the Liar's Club in Wisconsin, the year's winning lie told of a grandfather clock so old that the shadow of its swinging pendulum had worn a hole through the back of the clock.

In the grandfather clock of the Grand Canyon that bit of fabricated fancy strikes very close to the truth. The shadowed places in the Canyon's depths--concealed nooks where sunlight never penetrates--shelter frost and ice which linger long after winter's storms have passed. The ice melts a bit by day, and refreezes at night. Its action breaks up the rocks, literally shaping the Canyon. In this greatest of all grandfather timepieces, the shadows have helped wear a bigger hole in the clock.

Time--as humans count it--is completely meaningless in Grand Canyon. Einstein must have wrestled with concepts such as one experiences here.

In the Canyon, for the first time perhaps, one can begin to get a tenuous handle on Einstein's Theory of Relativity. It can be the oddest--almost most insulting--description of the Grand Canyon that has ever been written, but this Time Clock of Eternity might be described in Einstein's four symbol equation $E=MC^2$. To the average lay person--and that definitely includes us--Einstein's theory, and the time factors involved in the Canyon's formation, are equally incapable of being comprehended.

Einstein's equation led eventually to the development of atomic power. Down here in the Canyon one is subtly conscious of a power far greater, far deeper, than the atom. One sees and feels, here, the power which is ultimate.

XXXIX

Life Begins at 80

1984

Turning four score is an adventure; it needs special celebration. What better way than to spend a week of reminiscence and review surrounded by the scenes and challenges which have helped through the years to keep us physically fit, as well as mentally alert, aesthetically responsive, and spiritually attuned. In January of 1984 we celebrated Francis' 80th birthday at Grand Canyon.

Our close friends Don and Joyce, much younger than we, and who bear the Canyon's magical surname of *Harvey,* accompanied us on the festive occasion. They were newcomers to the Canyon; our week of review became, for them, a whole series of neophites' initiation rites. During our time at — and below — the South Rim we tested portions of five major Canyon trails — the Kaibab, Bright Angel, Hermit, River, and Tonto. We walked the trail along South Rim and tried to absorb the thousand square miles of choice scenery spread before us. We experienced one of the best green flashes we have ever witnessed (see Chapter 36). So far as we have thus far been able to determine, this may have been only the second sighting of that phenomenon in the

279

Canyon's history. We again took our favorite hike down the steep South Kaibab Trail, for an overnight stay at Phantom Ranch, with the nine and one-half mile return next day on the Bright Angel Trail made adventurous by a coating of ice along much of the last quarter mile. This was the first time we had hiked to the river in mid-winter; the seasonal decorations were like icing on a birthday cake.

At Indian Gardens there had been more icing for the cake; a chance meeting with Bruce Aiken, who for years has been living with his wife and children in the Canyon's depths — at Roaring Springs, where Bruce has supervised the pumping station which supplies water to the Rim. Imagine living in — not at, but *in* — Grand Canyon. He is a geologist, an artist, and — along with his wife — a teacher of their three small children.

The Canyon, in Francis' birthday month, has a special charm, not only for its cloak of winter climate but because of the quiet, and at times the almost complete solitude, which the lack of summer crowds makes possible. One evening we went to a ranger lecture attended by only 14 persons besides ourselves. With a group that small we were able to get acquainted. Those 14 people came — variously — from Australia, Equador, England, South Africa, Nepal, Saskatchewan, and from Kansas, Iowa, Michigan, Minnesota, Ohio and California. Grand Canyon's outreach is worldwide!

A young ranger couple — as fine an example of dedicated park personnel as we have come across — hosted a birthday party for Francis in their snug little home back in the pines from the Rim. Mike and Ann Swartz both are seasonal interpretive rangers at Yavapai Geology Museum, perched on the Canyon's edge. Their job is to explain the significance of the Canyon for the visitors in terms of geology, human and natural history.

Mike's season of lectures had ended shortly before our arrival. We had taken such a liking to him, and he to us that — on his own time — he accompanied us on the round trip hike to Phantom. For us it was an exciting two day absorption of knowledge — and a renewal of a friendship. The only way that life can really begin at 80 is by reaching out to new and vital young friendships, and seeking out new and worthwhile experiences.

On their Canyon hike to the river celebrating Francis' 80th birthday, he and Helen admire some 15-foot-long icicles.

The climax of Francis' birthday experience came at the bestowing of gifts. This was not at the actual birthday party itself — although the whole week long affair was a continuing celebration of love and life. The bestowing of gifts came in those magic moments after we had topped out, terminating our struggle up the final torturous switchbacks on the trail.

As we relaxed in Bright Angel Lodge, Mike produced a colorful brochure which had just come off the presses. "Grand Gifts for a Grand Canyon" was its theme. In a desire, with an ever more limited budget, to expand the Canyon's outreach to its nearly three million annual visitors, the National Park Service is inviting everyone to share in the Canyon's physical upkeep and well-being.

Mike excitedly opened the ten page brochure. He ran a finger along the descriptive list of suggested donations.

"We didn't make our gift at the party," he explained. "Now is the best time. Now we know the spot on the Canyon's trails which you love the most."

Mike's finger rested on the description of one particular gift, labeled "Adopt a Trail." Maintaining these Canyon trails, which have meant and will continue to mean so much in our lives, costs money — approximately 80¢ a foot per year. The Swartz' were "giving" us — or making it possible for us to "adopt" — 30 feet of the Bright Angel Trail, near the upper part of the Corkscrew. This is the section that traverses the marble-like polished rock which through the action of the ages has been metamorphized from dullness to grandeur. Years ago Helen mentally chose this strip of rejuvenated beauty as the most vital symbolic feature of the Canyon's entire trail system. We have shared its symbolic message with a thousand friends.

Helen says she always feels the eternal spirit here, putting the finishing touches on this exquisite Canyon — a rainbow in flowing marble. She echoes Walt Whitman's words:

Spirit that form'd this scene,
These tumbled rock-piles grim and red . . .
These gorges, turbulent-clear streams, this
    naked freshness,
These formless wild arrays, for reasons of their own,
I know thee, savage spirit — we have communed together,

For years Helen has loved this section of Bright Angel Trail. As a present on Francis' 80th birthday, Mike and Ann Swartz helped the Lines "adopt" it.

Mine too such wild arrays, for reasons of their own;
. . . thou that revelest here — spirit that
   form'd this scene,
They have remember'd thee.[1]

This strip of trail was the Swartz' "gift" to Francis, which he will of course share with Helen forever. In Francis' name, symbolically, that bit of trail will be improved and kept in repair, so that the visitors who pass over it may tread in safety as they absorb the metamorphic message. We and the Swartz' have made a pledge to fund the maintenance of that portion of trail, at least until the year 2000.

Our guests the Harvey's were newcomers to all this splendor. Don had never visited Grand Canyon before. Joyce had once passed by here briefly as a teenager. She had never done the type of hiking required to descend to the Colorado River and back.

Although Joyce didn't tell us until it was over, that struggle up the final mile of ice-encrusted trail to the last tunnel, which was within a few yards of topping out — that last stretch tried her endurance to the limit. She said she could not have negotiated even one more switchback. Bravely she had endured to the tunnel and the top, and that was it.

We dedicated that tunnel to Joyce. It is a tunnel almost in name only — only 15 or 20 feet long. But vital. It is a clearly visible goal for those struggling toward the top.

Don and Joyce made us a "gift" of the portion of trail passing through that tunnel, and of a couple of hundred more feet leading toward the top. Thus we become, symbolically, agents in its maintenance for the benefit of the millions who come this way. Comparatively few of the three million annual visitors descend — either by mule or on foot — to the Canyon depths. But hundreds of thousands of them walk the few feet down to the first tunnel. Other donors may also choose to "adopt" that particular portion of the trail, which will be good, for all the boots and shoes of those visitors from every corner of the world will cause it to be in need of constant repair. Now we will be a more intimate part of that process. Through the gifts from our friends we have adopted two portions of the Canyon trails.[2]

Sixty-one years ago Francis realized that the Canyon was far more than its physical features alone. In our hundreds of visits here, we have sensed that there is not only an inner gorge, but an inner meaning — an inner message — to this bold creation. The Canyon is not only physically deep, it has a depth of symbolism which reaches the heart. Its aesthetic, intellectual and spiritual challenges stir one's blood just as surely as the physical adventures which it affords.

The "Chariots of Fire" motion picture contains a statement by an Olympic running champion: "So where does the power come from to see the race to the end? From within! God made me for a purpose."

Grand Canyon is more than a colossal chasm. There is reality in its designation as a "divine abyss." On the Rim one senses its power. Down in the depths, one feels and experiences that power. Just as with a person, this power of the Canyon comes from within.

As Bruce Aiken's wife, Mary, said after one of her many nighttime walks in the Canyon's depths: "You can feel God. I never really knew God until I walked down here at night. I mean the power, the glory, all that stuff. You can feel God, sense His presense."[3]

God made Grand Canyon for a purpose. On Francis' 80th birthday party, this miracle chasm conveyed to us even greater and fresher meanings.

It's a Grand Canyon.

XL

A Two Billionth
Birthday Party! A.D. 2000

2000

A time of special wonder and awe will soon be at hand, when visitors to Grand Canyon who penetrate to its depths--either physically or visually--will see the Vishnu schist rocks of that magnificent granite gorge preparing to celebrate their two billionth year of rugged existence.

Park rangers and geologists have for some time been saying, "The Vishnu schist at the bottom of Grand Canyon is approximately two billion years old."

An approximation is not enough. We feel it would be desirable that a definite date for that two billionth birthday celebration be established. In the first edition of this book we had set it for 1990. But the year 2000 seems more appropriate. That is a watershed date, easily remembered. We may be off by a few years--who can say?--but we are taking it on ourselves to proclaim that May 1, in the year 2000, should be declared the official two billionth birthday of those serrated walls in the granite gorge.

Plans can begin now for dedicating that year to fostering and preserving the Canyon's wonders. The year 2000 can be a time of celebration--but not of frivolous trivialities. No fireworks will be needed; the Canyon will provide its own magical displays of lightning, accompanied by drumbeats of rumbling thunder.

Decorations of Japanese garden lanterns will be unnecessary; Grand Canyon has a long-term arrangement with the night sky to hang out a complete canopy of stars, and occasionally a moon. By day, the sky will spread cumulus banners and cirrus streamers over the scene.

No confetti please; nature has already arranged for that. Millions of pounds of it, shaped like snowflakes, will filter down to make the narrow granite gorge seem like Broadway under a snowstorm of ticker tape.

There need be no birthday presents. Granite gorge has its own gifts of rocks which shine like diamonds and sapphires and rubies.

What is required, more than *celebration*, is *dedication*--a dedication to the proposition that the Canyon will endure. Not necessarily another billion years but--more to the point--another thousand. Humankind can easily upset the entire process.

A dam could wipe much of it out in a decade. A bill has been before congress to create an enormous lake in the Canyon's depths. Thousands of tourists, entering by boat, could enjoy leisurely closeup examinations of the Canyon walls. Environmentalists responded: "Should we also flood the Sistine Chapel so tourists can get nearer the ceiling?"

Uncontrolled tourism along the Rim could desecrate much of the Canyon's grandeur in one generation. Sensible restraints are needed.

Unregulated coal-burning plants could further dull its sparkle and pollute its air.

Grand Canyon's birthday celebration in 2000 should be, to coin a phrase, a time for concentrated consecration.

The authors of this book will have been wed 72 years on May 1, 2000. Francis will be 97 a few days after that year terminates.

Even if we don't live that long, physically--who knows?-- we'll be there in spirit. If you promise to come with a feeling of reverence and awe, and tread gently as though you were walking on sacred ground (for that is what the Canyon really is) then we invite you to join us. We'll see you May 1, A.D. 2000, to help pay homage to this life-enhancing miracle--Grand Canyon!

XLI

PS

This must surely be one of the few books which contains a postscript. This is added not only after the book was written, but after it was set in type and partly printed.

One month and two days before we were to head into Grand Canyon on our May 1, 56th wedding anniversary hike, Helen had a ruptured appendix, an emergency operation, and a case of peritonitis. For 19 hours she was in the hospital's intensive care unit.

Then she started an amazing recovery. In a week she was home. Soon she could take short walks — first a few blocks, then a mile. Twenty-seven days after her operation she walked the steep up-and-down two miles which we regularly take three times a week.

To have made the 20 mile round trip grueling hike to Grand Canyon's Phantom Ranch, just one week later, would have been pushing things too much. But Helen had a birthday coming up on May 24. We had celebrated Francis' 80th birthday with a Grand Canyon hike; why not honor Helen likewise?

We were able to get reservations at Supai in the lower end of

Grand Canyon, at their new Havasupai Lodge. While this hike would be longer than to Phantom Ranch, it would be less steep. We made the eight miles down on her birthday, next day did the six mile round trip to the three magic waterfalls, including the arduous chain-and-tunnel descent to the base of Mooney Falls, then the eight miles back out.

The doctors — and many others — are calling Helen the "Strong Lady." A longtime Phoenix, Arizona newspaper publisher, Robert Creighton, wrote us, referring to the fact of Helen's birthplace being in that state's Gila County (pronounced "Hela").

"We are of course delighted — but not surprised — to know of Helen's great recovery from her operation. Gals from 'Hee-lee Countee' are gristle tough and it takes more than a busted appendix (or even four or five holes from a 44') to down them. Some of the finest cutthroats in the West came from there and she should be proud of her geographical heritage."

Francis has always been considered the seasoned hiker in our family, carrying the larger pack and doing all he could to aid Helen on the hardest stretches. Now she has gained a reputation which surpasses his. He made her a special birthday card, inscribed: "You've come a long way, Baby!"

Supai itself had come a long way also, since our last visit. The new lodge — available for occupancy although it would not be officially dedicated until a week after our departure — was a creative architectural expression which blended with its ancient red wall surroundings. We found it hard to realize that all this air-conditioned luxury, these bath facilities in which solar water heating played a large role, these spacious rooms with double beds and handsome furniture, all had been carried down from the outside world either by helicopter or by pack animal. The young men in charge — Havasupai Indians educated in the village school — were soft-spoken, friendly, efficient.

The new lodge had prompted a remodeling of the village cafe. The camping area, stretching along the stream below the village, had been enlarged. Supai, the only Indian settlement within Grand Canyon, was being clothed anew.

And the waterfalls. Where Navajo Falls had tumbled down in isolation we found, instead, nine shimmering cascades, of as many different shapes and sizes, all churning downward over a long vegetation-clothed escarpment. Some had their individual rainbows. Some plunged down straight as arrows. Others split, regrouped, and shot sideways as they met projecting rocks. Havasu Falls, farther along, cascaded with half again as much magnificent power as it had displayed at our former visits. Mooney Falls churned with nearly twice its former volume.

As we followed the stream between these falls it divided, its branches creating water wonderlands beneath the trees. At one place there were deep mysterious pools lined with green finery which swayed like grasses blown by wind. Heavy snowfalls — somewhere — had fed new life and urgency into these magic waters of Supai, in Grand Canyon's western depths.

Their music rose upward and expanded. The towering escarpments caught the sounds and tossed them back to us. We shivered in delight as we imagined what they might be saying. This was our beloved Grand Canyon speaking.

We absorbed its secret message.

Notes

Chapter 1   Honeymoon Chariot
1. Only in much later years did we learn that Peach Springs had been the place from which, in the 1880s and 90s, hardy travelers had left the railroad and ridden that 20 miles by horse or stage to view Grand Canyon's lower reaches. We were glad that we were ignorant, then, of these facts. Had we visited the Canyon above Peach Springs, we would probably not have gone in to make our early acquaintance with the more noted Bright Angel area.

Chapter 9   The Music of Tonto Plateau
1. This is variously called Tonto Plateau or Tonto Platform. The two names are interchangeable.
2. Irvin S. Cobb, in ROUGHING IT DELUXE from Saturday Evening Post, June 7 and 28, 1983. (Printed in THE GRAND CANYON, edited and copyrighted by Paul Schullery, 1981. Colorado Associated University Press. Page 151.

Chapter 12   Rescue Below the Rim
1. Cedar Ridge is misnamed. The trees here are the Utah juniper.

Chapter 14   Coasting Canyonward
1. In 1983, by coincidence, Francis was able to make contact with the ranger who had, in 1925, told him about the deer drive. Now retired, he is R. B. McAllister of Salt Lake City.

Chapter 15   North Rim Magic
1. Francis — and sometimes Helen — took our motion pictures on lecture trips to the auditoriums of the major cities of the United States and Canada, showing them personally before more than a million persons.

Chapter 19   By Jeep to Toroweap
1. Edwin Corle's LISTEN, BRIGHT ANGEL page 298. Copyright, 1946, by Edwin Corle. Published by Duell, Sloan and Pearle, New York.
2. Ibid, pages 297-298
3. EARTH FEATURES AND THEIR MEANING, by Hobbs, published 1912 by The Macmillan Co. N.Y.

Chapter 20   Grand Canyon Retreat
1. MAN WITH A SONG, SOME MAJOR AND MINOR NOTES IN THE LIFE OF FRANCIS OF ASSISI by Francis and Helen Line. Published by Doubleday (Image imprint) 1982.
2. NO TURNING BACK, by Polingaysi, published and copyrighted, 1964, University of New Mexico Press.

Chapter 22   Adventure by Night
1. Gathering wood and building fires is now prohibited in Grand Canyon, since the great number of hikers and campers would soon deplete the supply. Wood is important in the Canyon's ecology, providing food and shelter for wildlife, and in many other ways.
2. The Rim to Rim hiking distance is approximately 21 miles. With our sidetrip to Ribbon Falls, and our walk from the South Kaibab trailhead out to the highway, it was at least 22 miles. It seemed like 30.

Chapter 23   Cow Pasture Landing
1. See Note 2, Chapter 22

Chapter 25   Red Rock Trail to Supai
1. EXPLORE GRAND CANYON by Felton O. Gamble. published by Northland Press, Flagstaff, Arizona. Copyright, 1971 by Felton O. Gamble. Page 19.

Chapter 26   The Legend of Havasu Canyon
1. "Topocoba" is spelled in several different ways.

Chapter 28   Notebook Journey on Rim and Trail
1. From Thoreau's essay on "Walking," Harvard Classics, Vol. 28, page 395.

Chapter 30 The Cemetery Is a History Book
1. Research for this chapter was aided by various references from IN THE HOUSE OF STONE AND LIGHT, by J. Donald Hughes, copyright 1978 by Grand Canyon Natural History Association.

Chapter 31 The Great Unknown
1. IN THE HOUSE OF STONE AND LIGHT, by J. Donald Hughes, copyright 1978 by Grand Canyon Natural History Association. Page 20.

2. GRAND CANYON, AN ANTHOLOGY, compiled and text copyrighted 1978 by Bruce Babbitt. Published by Northland Press, Flagstaff, Arizona. Page 21.

3. THE GRAND CANYON, edited and copyrighted, 1981 by Paul Schullery. Colorado Associated University Press. Pages 123-124.

4. Joseph Christmas Ives "Report Upon the Colorado River of the West; Explored in 1857 and 1859'', Washington Government Printing Office, 1861. Reprinted on page 28 IN THE HOUSE OF STONE AND LIGHT, published and copyrighted 1978 by Grand Canyon Natural History Association.

5. ibid.

6. George M. Wheeler, "Report Upon United States Geographical Surveys West of the One Hundredth Meridian,'' Vol. 1: Geographical Report, Washington Government Printing Office, 1889, page 168. Reprinted on page 38 IN THE HOUSE OF STONE AND LIGHT.

7. The National Geographic Magazine, July 1978, page 16.

8. GRAND CANYON, AN ANTHOLOGY, compiled and text copyrighted 1978 by Bruce Babbitt. Pages 59-60.

9. ibid, page 57

10. John T. McCutcheon, "Doing the Grand Canyon" (Kansas City, Mo. Fred Harvey, 1909). Reprinted on pages 111-112 in THE GRAND CANYON, edited and copyrighted by Paul Schullery, 1981. Colorado Associated University Press.

Chapter 32 "Imagine . . . Imagine . . . Imagine"
1. From MIDNIGHT ON THE DESERT, by J. B. Priestley. Published by William Heinemann, Ltd. 1937. Reprinted on page 103, GRAND CANYON, AN ANTHOLOGY, compiled and text copyrighted, 1978 by Bruce Babbitt. Published by Northland Press, Flagstaff, Arizona.

2. From Owen Wister's preface to THROUGH THE GRAND CANYON FROM WYOMING TO MEXICO, by E. L. Kolb, copyright 1914 by Macmillan Publishing Co., renewed by Ellsworth L. Kolb. Reprinted on page 104 in THE GRAND CANYON, edited and copyrighted by Paul Schullery, 1981. Colorado Associated University Press.

3. John T. McCutcheon, "Doing the Grand Canyon" (Kansas City, Mo. Fred Harvey, 1909). Reprinted on page 112 in THE GRAND CANYON, edited and copyrighted by Paul Schullery, 1981. Colorado Associated University Press.

4. Charles F. Lummis — page 191 in Edwin Corle's LISTEN BRIGHT ANGEL, published by Duell, Sloan & Pearce, copyrighted 1946 by Edwin Corle.

5. Haniel Long in PIÑON COUNTRY published by Duell, Sloan & Pearce, 1941. Reprinted on page 129, GRAND CANYON, AN ANTHOLOGY, compiled and text copyrighted 1978 by Bruce Babbitt.

6. Irvin Cobb ROUGHING IT DELUXE, published by George H. Duran Co. 1913. Reprinted on pages 93 and 94, GRAND CANYON, AN ANTHOLOGY, compiled and text copyrighted 1978 by Bruce Babbitt.

7. ibid ROUGHING IT DELUXE, reprinted on page 95 of GRAND CANYON, AN ANTHOLOGY, compiled and text copyrighted 1978 by Bruce Babbitt. Published by Northland Press, Flagstaff, Arizona.

8. ibid ROUGHING IT DELUXE, reprinted on page 95.

9. GRAND CANYON, AN ANTHOLOGY, compiled and text copyrighted 1978 by Bruce Babbitt. Northland Press, Flagstaff, Arizona, page 57.

10. LISTEN BRIGHT ANGEL, by Edwin Corle. Published by Duell, Sloan & Pearce, copyrighted 1946 by Edwin Corle, page 191.

11. ibid. page 191.

12. ibid. page 192.

13. ibid. page 303.

14. ibid. page 300.

Chapter 35   Hiking the Inner Trails
1. THE WILDERNESS WORLD OF THE GRAND CANYON, Ann and Myron Sutton. Published by J. B. Lippincott Co., Philadelphia and New York, 1971. Text copyrighted 1970 by Ann and Myron Sutton, page 121.
2. ibid. page 56.
3. ibid. page 56.
4. ibid. pages 114 and 208.
5. ibid. page 114.
6. W. E. Garrett, The National Geographic Magazine, July 1978, page 17.
7. ibid. page 23.
8. From THE WILDERNESS WORLD OF THE GRAND CANYON, Ann and Myron Sutton. Published by J. B. Lippincott Co., Philadelphia and New York, 1971. Text copyrighted 1970 by Ann and Myron Sutton.
9. Irvin Cobb ROUGHING IT DELUXE, published by George H. Duran Co. 1913. Reprinted on page 97 of GRAND CANYON, AN ANTHOLOGY, compiled and text copyrighted 1978 by Bruce Babbitt. Northland Press, Flagstaff, Arizona.
10. Irvin S. Cobb ROUGHING IT DELUXE. Reprinted on page 94 in GRAND CANYON, AN ANTHOLOGY, compiled and text copyrighted 1978 by Bruce Babbitt. Northland Press, Flagstaff, Arizona.

Chapter 39   Life Begins at 80
1. From the poem "Spirit that form'd this scene" by Walt Whitman, in his LEAVES OF GRASS.
2. For practical purposes, monies donated for trail maintenance cannot be used just for specific segments of a trail, but with sufficient donations all major trails can be maintained.
3. Arizona Highways, April 1981. page 43. Article by Bill McClellan. Copyright 1981 by the Arizona Department of Transportation.

The authors, Francis and Helen Line.

About the Authors

For forty years Francis and Helen Line produced travel-adventure motion pictures, with which Francis lectured personally before more than a million persons in auditoriums across the United States and Canada. They also made and distributed documentary educational films which are shown today in school classrooms, film libraries, and universities in every state of the Union. For the last fourteen years they have turned to writing, together or separately having written six published books.

Francis is a graduate of the University of Michigan's department of journalism (magna cum laude), a member of the Los Angeles Adventurers Club, Phi Beta Kappa, and--until distance made attendance impracticable--of the New York Explorers and the Circumnavigators Clubs.

Helen, reared on a four-hundred-square-mile Arizona cattle ranch, studied home economics and nutrition in college. Her dietary knowledge and skills--together with other factors-- have helped keep them in the physical condition required for strenuous Grand Canyon hiking, including the 20 mile round trip foray to the Canyon's Colorado River to celebrate their 50th wedding anniversary--and similar hikes every anniversary since.

They have a daughter, three grandchildren, and one great grandson, all of whom are carrying on the hiking tradition. Their granddaughter Krista is a marathon runner and helped carry the 1984 "Olympic Torch."

On January 15, 1975 the Los Angeles Metropolitan YMCA presented the first Martin Luther King, Jr. Human Dignity Award to Francis and Helen, in recognition of outstanding service rendered to the youth of Watts, and to the Navajo Indians, on whose reservation the Lines lived for two years as they produced a documentary motion picture there.

In 1987 they received the Remarkable Senior Award at the Los Angeles Convention Center. Their 59th wedding anniversary hike in Grand Canyon, plus involvement in social projects, won them this award.

OTHER BOOKS FROM WIDE HORIZONS PRESS

SHEEP, STARS, AND SOLITUDE:
ADVENTURE SAGA OF A WILDERNESS TRAIL
by Francis Raymond Line

The experiences of following 2000 sheep over one of the wildest trails in America are recounted in this "Arizona Walden." Line first wrote up the trek for *National Geographic Magazine* and *Arizona Highways*. The book combines adventure, philosophy, humor, nature, spirituality, and ecology in a true story of unique beauty.

"A gentle classic which warms the soul while contributing to western literature." Stanley W. Paher, *Southwest Bookshelf*

"The U.S. Government and the National Geographic Magazine have recognized the simple wisdom of Line's story. It is enjoyable and rewarding." *Small Press Book Review*

165 pages, 45 photographs, softcover, $8.95
ISBN: 0-938109-01-2   Library of Congress: 86-11154

AWAY FROM THE CROWD
ADVENTURE TRAVELS IN THE WEST
by Adrienne Knute

This all-season guide leads you to unusual camping and vacation spots filled with solitude and beauty in California, Arizona, Utah, Nevada, Mexico. There are hints for pre-trip planning and a chapter on easy camp meals. From desert waterfalls, to sacred Indian mountains, there's a perfect trip for you.

"These places sound like fun." *Books of the Southwest,* University of Arizona.

132 pages, 18 maps, photographs, softcover, $7.95
ISBN: 0-938109-01-4   Library of Congress: 86-9101

FOOT BY FOOT THROUGH THE USA
by Winfield and Francis Line

A high adventure odyssey to every state in the Union. Two teenage boys, in the adolescent years of America's highway travel, set out to learn about their country in the most intimate way possible--hiking, catching rides, and working their way for over a year. This true story takes you on a journey back in time through a historic and scenic USA. It's a combination of humor and history, geography and grit. A must on every American's reading list.

"This book should be a 'must' reading for all students in high school." Mr. Yong Keun Cha, Federal Aviation Authority, Washington, D.C.

"A delightful account of that trip." Dick Kleiner, *The Desert Sun*, Palm Springs, California

"Their adventure provides an entertaining way to read about an earlier time in America's history." Friends of the Library, Howell, Michigan

312 pages, 77 photos, 15 maps, softcover, $8.95
ISBN: 0-938109-03-0 Library of Congress: 86-28939

****

You may order these books by mail from Wide Horizons Press. Please include $1 for one book, 50 cents for each additional book, for postage and handling. California residents add 6% tax.

Prices are subject to change without notice.

SPECIAL DISCOUNTS: We offer a 10% discount for orders over $25; 20% for orders over $50.

BOOKSELLERS: Please request a copy of our discount schedule.

See next page for ordering information.
Send to:
Wide Horizons Press
13 Meadowsweet
Irvine, CA 92715

Ordering Information

GRAND CANYON LOVE STORY $8.95

SHEEP, STARS, AND SOLITUDE $8.95

AWAY FROM THE CROWD $7.95

FOOT BY FOOT THROUGH THE USA $8.95

Take 10% discount for orders over $25; 20% for orders over $50.

Figure discounts before adding tax and postage.

Add $1 postage and handling for 1 book; 50 cents for each additional book.

California residents add 6% sales tax.
Prices are subject to change without notice.

SATISFACTION GUARANTEED. You may return the books for a full refund if you are not entirely pleased.

Additional information and brochures available upon request to:

WIDE HORIZONS PRESS
13 Meadowsweet
Irvine, CA 92715

see other side